WHAT OTHERS ARE SAYING ABOUT THIS BOOK

Simplify is a crucial read for those working in High Performance and Leadership. Richard has brilliantly and succinctly captured what it takes to achieve mastery at the highest level in both sport and life. There are so many insightful take outs: a focus on improvement rather than winning, uncovering strengths rather than fixing weaknesses, finetuning the system through subtraction not addition and relentlessly reflecting. Effective questions throughout the text help to frame concepts of individual and team competitive advantage. *Simplify* is a stimulating read that provokes meaningful action along the pathway to exceptional performance.

– Katie Sadleir, GM Women's Rugby, World Rugby.

I have had the good fortune of knowing Richard for close to twenty years. I always thought I was pretty good at keeping things simple and then I met Richard. It was clear that I was the novice and Richard was the expert. Richard, through his book, *Simplify*, has done it again. His insights have provided a guiding light on a couple of areas that have been puzzling us at the Padres. It has enabled us to sharpen our thinking, remove clutter and adapt our system to provide us with a greater chance of success. Like me, if you are serious about taking your game to another level, then *Simplify* is a must-read.

r, Director Player Health and 'ormance, San Diego Padres.

Whether in business or in sport, applying an agile approach is critical to unlocking and unblocking potential. Take the smallest part of the best idea, be willing to experiment and should it fail –do it fast. In *Simplify*, Richard explains so clearly how great coaches focus on creating learners and leaders who, in turn, deliver achievement and fulfilment. Where to start and how to break down the complexity are all too often the barriers to being the best one can be. The complexity of how to be your best has now been removed in this must-read book.

– Duane Kale, Vice President International Paralympic Committee, Paralympian.

Richard had me from the opening sentence and it simply grew from there. In our work in broadcasting and analytical graphics, we are part of many of the great events in the world (PGA golf, Americas Cup, Formula 1, International cricket, Major league baseball etc.). My company, Animation Research, analyses high performance on the world stage and the insights within the book Simplify captures so succinctly how the best can achieve world class results. To have a book pull these insights together is a competitive advantage for both performers and business. When you decide that you are going to play on the world stage then it is a given that you need to surround yourself with a world class system and world class people who share that vision and see no limits. Richard has superbly captured what that means and how it can be actioned and achieved to make the complex simple and let the results look after themselves. Read *Simplify* for your performance advantage in sport, business and life!

– Sir Ian Taylor, Emmy award winning sport analysis and broadcasting, MD Animation Research Ltd.

Such a timely book for the world, following eighteen months of disruption where many routines have had to adapt and overcome in a new environment. This book breaks down performance in a simple way and provides tools to re-examine your performance principles and either design a new system or redesign an existing system. It's a must-read for any high-performance players.

– Danny Klima, Director, Abu Dhabi Motorsport Management.

Having spent 27 years in Olympic level sport and knowing first-hand how complex this environment is, I read Richard's book with much interest. *Simplify* is a fantastic reference book, both enthralling and insightful. It really brings high value for those aspiring for higher performance. Richard has skills, experience and a human dimension that makes him unique in our industry. He has deeply simplified the complexity of high performance matters to uncover core principles we can use in our work as leaders and performers. His book is essential reading for anyone aiming for higher performance through concrete elements and experiences. Richard lays out a map across nine key principles to help us simplify and understand the opportunities in front of us and lift the game! Read this book for immediate value to your world, challenges and objectives.

– Jean-Laurent Bourquin, CEO AdviSport, Geneva, Switzerland.

Richard understands the keys to performance and shows how the basics must be clear before any real high performance can be achieved. *Simplify* is an incredible guide to performance leadership: leading your system and leading performance in you and others. It will help you build deep belief and confidence in your action. Read *Simplify* to find your highest performing self.

– Tanya Dubnicoff, 3x Olympian, World Champion and Olympic Coach.

High performance is an often misunderstood term. In my experience those who have the ability to simplify its meaning and then adapt provide direction to focus on where you can make the most effective and sustainable gains. *Simplify* is key in figuring out this critical process. Read this book to uncover your performance advantage!

– Mike Hesson, Director of Cricket Royal Challengers Bangalore (Indian Premier League), Former Blackcaps Coach 2012-2018.

Wow, what a great book! Richard Young's book, *Simplify*, is a goldmine of insights about high performance. Based on his extensive and successful experience as an athlete, coach, and performance improvement expert, Richard shares many important secrets of success in such a clear and practical way. As I read, I kept filling up pages with notes that I will refer to often. Richard explains that too many performers complicate performance, thinking that adding techniques will improve performance, when it most often detracts from high performance. Those who truly understand and have confidence in their system will eliminate (subtract) non-essentials, and thereby streamline performance. If you want to become better at whatever you do, and want to help others do likewise, then *Simplify* is a must-read and a must-use book.

– Dr Dean R. Spitzer, International expert on performance measurement, Author of eight books including the bestselling *Transforming Performance Measurement.*

Simplify is a must read for insights into creating high performance. The book delivers unique actionable thoughts of how to unpack systems that will help athletes and performance groups to have impact on high end performance. *Simplify* will give you insights that usually come much later in an athlete's development. You now have the opportunity to get ahead in this game. You will also learn the secret to finding clear language when communicating performance tactics and techniques. Richard has presented critical information to accelerate performance faster and simpler. This book is a vital read for a head-start.

– Per Lundstam, Alpine Sport Science Director, US Ski & Snowboard, Former Director of Athlete Performance, Red Bull.

SIMPLIFY

SIMPLIFY

A HIGH PERFORMANCE PLAYBOOK TO WIN THE REAL GAME

RICHARD YOUNG PHD

Published by Richard Young

First published in 2021, Dunedin, New Zealand

Copyright © Richard Young

www.simplify2perform.com

Saint Clair, Dunedin, New Zealand

Disclaimer

The material in this publication is of the nature of general comment only and does not represent professional advice. It is not intended to provide specific guidance for particular circumstances, and it should not be relied on as the basis for any decision to take action or not to take action on any matter which it covers. Readers should obtain professional advice where appropriate, before making any such decision. To the maximum extent permitted by law, the author and publisher disclaim all responsibility and liability to any person, arising directly or indirectly from any person taking or not taking action based on the information in this publication.

All inquiries should be made to the author.

Edited by Jenny Magee

Designed and typeset in Australia by BookPOD

Printed in New Zealand by PHPrint

ISBN: 978-0-473-56470-4 (paperback)

ISBN: 978-0-473-56474-2 (e-book)

To Donna and our beautiful children Oliver, Gracie, Emily-Rose and Leo. That is the game that matters.

ACKNOWLEDGEMENTS

It has been a privilege to be involved with high performance over so many years. I acknowledge the collective intelligence of that worldwide community with whom I have had the privilege to meet, work with and learn from. They have made this book possible.

I have also had the great privilege over many years to meet and learn from a team of world experts who changed my thinking about sport and performance; Hubert and Stuart Dreyfus, Patricia Benner, Robert Fritz, Peter Senge, John Edwards, Brendan Spillane, Paul Chippendale, Matt Church, Dean Spitzer and Sir Ian Taylor.

The support of my family through highs and lows has been the rock in the sea.

My community of Thought Leaders has inspired me to accelerate personally and share messages to help others lift and clear their way.

My outstanding editor, Jenny Magee, who always had a smile and provided strong, creative support. And I appreciate the early steer on the creative direction from Michael Levine.

My business manager, Holly Grimmer, for logistical support to make things happen.

To you, a current or future high performer with this book in your hand, I want to acknowledge your potential and hope you find something here to lighten and accelerate your step!

FOREWORD

It is my pleasure to write the foreword for such a valuable book for the global community of future and current high performers.

After more than forty years in high performance sport, working in numerous systems around the world, I know first-hand how complex this environment can be. To optimise performance, we need to know the simple truth about what matters most, and the insights in this book are vital pointers.

At the 1984 Olympics, I won two gold medals, both with world records, because of great coaching and a performance system. Dr Jeno Tihany was my coach, mentor and our bond was deeper than sport, as he clearly understood the value of connecting me to a system that worked for me.

Since then, I have made my career as an executive in sport in Canada, Australia and New Zealand by focusing on improving international performance through individualised high performance systems.

While a performance system sounds like an abstract concept, it is simply how you do what you do and why you do it that way. It is the medal behind the medal. It supports personal performance in sport and beyond to family life and service to others. The learning is greater than the medal and carries on well after sporting careers have ended.

I had the pleasure of working with Richard when I was CEO of High Performance Sport New Zealand. He understands systems for exceptional performance better than anyone. Richard was responsible for performance gains through evidence and system growth that could be easily understood and used by coaches, athletes and performance staff across dozens of sports. His work worked.

Richard simplifies performance insights to make them directly applicable to the context of any performance. The insights in this book are important tools to find competitive advantage and accelerate.

Reading this book has also been a fascinating journey of recollection into my own performance and leadership history. High performance is a game of learning. If you have a system, this book can help you tune and polish it. If you don't yet have a system, this book is the road map you need. It simplifies the complex so you can lift and accelerate performance.

This is the primary focus for those of us who work to support others' performance – to help current and future experts in high performance know why and how and accelerate.

Competitive advantage comes from the quality of the system you are in. As Richard writes, if you are not clear on your system and what works best, you will be in motion without progress. There is no time to waste in high performance; quality counts most.

The principles underpinning *Simplify* will create a competitive advantage in your performance context. I hope you enjoy the learning and accelerate.

– Alex Baumann, CEO Swimming Australia
and former CEO High Performance Sport NZ,
Double Olympic gold medallist and
former double world record holder.

TABLE OF CONTENTS

THE QUEST BEGINS

The Puzzle

Duff Gibson was a wrestler in high school. He was a far better fighter than me – stronger, with more stamina and better technique.

My sport was cycling, and I worked my way into the Canadian team for the 1988 Olympics. At the first team meeting in Seoul, I was tackled from behind and wrestled to the ground. It was Duff – there, not as a wrestler, but as a future youth Olympian. After a hug, he said, 'I will get to the Olympics, and I will win.'

Clear and confident, he asked me to coach him in cycling when we got home. I was still racing, so couldn't do so, but I watched Duff's name move up the cycling ranks over the next few years.

Then I heard he had moved into rowing and was nationally ranked.

In 1992 I had the opportunity to do a PhD in Calgary, where Duff, now a nationally ranked speedskater, also lived. With his Olympic dream burning bright, Duff had switched sports again. And, once more, he made the national team.

I have never seen anyone train harder, smarter or with more commitment. His whole essence was pointed to the Olympic performance. Duff didn't just follow a training programme; he created a performance system he could use in any context.

Next, Duff saw an opportunity in bobsleigh and became one of the top drivers in the country. At the same time, the sport of skeleton racing was evolving and added to the Olympics in 2002. Duff moved to skeleton, racing headfirst down steep tracks at speeds of up to 130 kilometres per hour. He applied his performance system to the new sport, winning the world championship in his third year, then taking the Olympic gold medal at Turino in 2006. At the age of 39, Duff was the oldest individual gold medallist in Winter Olympic history.

And then, having proved what he'd told me in Seoul, he retired.

Duff showed me that excellence comes from understanding and being grounded in your personal high performance system. That high performance means layering specialist skills and focusing on what matters. He taught me that knowing what works best for you enables success in new environments and adventures.

Moving between sports, Duff was never starting from zero. Ninety per cent of his effort went into finding and polishing his performance system, leaving ten per cent to adapt to a new context.

Inspired by Duff and his clear-sighted ability, I have spent thirty years focused on the performance systems behind people, teams and organisations.

Each of us can develop such a system. The purpose of high performance is not to be a great skeleton athlete, cyclist, sailor, hockey player or rugby captain, but to be a high performer in life. That is the real game.

High performance can feel like a giant complex puzzle that requires years of experimentation with no guarantee of a successful outcome. A win is more likely when the performance system is solved correctly to deliver a performance on precisely the right day. In sport, we call this the peak.

Performance is contextual – for some athletes, it means a medal, while for a coach, it may be the development of a new athlete. A scientist may find success through discovery and a leader through a high-performing team dynamic. Your win will have a deep meaning specific to you. You

High performance can feel like a giant complex puzzle that requires years of experimentation with no guarantee of a successful outcome.

will be busy trying to uncover and optimise your performance system.

My youngest son Leo arrived home from a class gift exchange at primary school with a bag of thousands of puzzle pieces. 'Dad,' he said, 'Can we build this puzzle?' 'Sure, what is the picture?' 'I don't know. There is no box, so let's just start.' We began by laying down the edges and corners, then finding pieces that went together. After several hours, Leo said, 'Wow, now I know why they put the picture on the box!'

For most people, this is exactly how high performance evolves – from a giant bag of puzzle pieces. Some pieces we know well, some we have seen others do, others we have read about, and many come from what we are told is the way to high performance. Our coach may tell us what the edges are (sleep and good nutrition). We may learn that the other teams are using plyometrics, but we don't know where it fits.

At first sight, the options seem overwhelming – and they are. There are so many books on high performance, training, mindset and nutrition that it is impossible to build one picture. And anyway, the pictures conflict. Each new approach, supplement or technique looks like an essential piece to add. We struggle to find the magic missing piece that holds it all together. Most athletes I have raced with, worked with and met are eager to add that crucial piece, but to do so, they must continually experiment to discover which elements work. The unseen picture grows more and more complicated.

And if that's not enough, we must also attend to the ticking stopwatches on the puzzle. The event is coming on a set day, time and place, and they can't be late. Many sports require a physical body that can handle training and recovery, and most athletes have only four to eight years at the highest level of their game.

Solving the puzzle is me telling my son, 'OK Leo, you need to finish this as fast as you can tonight because you won't be interested by next week.'

In some cases, best practice would be to find the box. While that approach is critical in fields such as engineering and the sciences, in high performance sport, fitting into someone else's picture of success can be too slow and too late. We need to uncover our own performance system first and build it quickly. Once it is clear, we will have our own best practice.

But to solve the unknown, we need best principles to build a performance system. Best principles beat best practice. It's like finding the corners and the edges first, as without them, there is no starting point.

Best principles beat best practice.

Performance and expertise are contextual. A violin virtuoso in a sail boat with no training is not an expert sailor. But with the right principles, likely found in their system of music expertise, the violinist can know where to start – or at least know what questions to ask.

That is where this book points – uncovering the principles of high performance systems to solve your own puzzle and create your own performance system. One that, as Duff discovered, you can carry into any environment. One that will give you the power to win the long game.

Throughout this book, we will explore principles and systems to uncover and simplify your own performance picture.

The book is in four parts.

In Part One, you'll explore the overall performance framework and its underlying principles to build your ecosystem for exceptional performance. We are all capable of exceptional performance, and the discovery begins here.

Part Two explains the priorities that exceptional performers have set for themselves. We explore how they move and realign their self-awareness, values, and conviction to achieve the extraordinary performances they are capable of.

In Part Three, we unpack how the wider team and supporters interact – together and with the performer. No exceptional performer does it alone. We explore their focus on rigorous honesty, why it matters to find and adhere to the right action and, finally, the delivery of flow through strategic simplification.

Part Four looks at three core system components; knowing the standard we must reach, collecting the right evidence to see progress, and building momentum to bring the desired future to reality and avoid performance oscillation.

Finally, in Part Five, we combine all the components to explore the ecosystem as a dashboard. You can use it to track your progress and identify key areas to polish and align. Here we bring your system into full view to enable exceptional performance in your world.

PART ONE

THE PERFORMANCE PRINCIPLES

CHAPTER ONE

THE DECISION

The game

A Canadian international figure skater was consumed with winning her place on the Olympic team. She trained harder than other skaters, and her hunger to win was an all-consuming drive. Unfortunately, that drive, particularly in artistic sports, can hamper the athlete's performance. Her efforts certainly deserved a place on the Olympic team, but her focus was more on winning than dancing, and that showed in her performances.

Following an injury, she gave up on making the Olympics. Without that pressure, she recovered and danced the best performances of her life for many more years. Once her love of learning to perform was unleashed, her dancing was all about expression and communication. By refocusing her attention, she fell in love with a new level of skating and won more competitions. She talked about the fundamental shift that followed her injury, moving from an environment that was competitive and win-focused to dancing for sheer joy and creativity.

I start conversations with high performers with one question: 'What is most important about high performance for you?' In their answers, I am listening for their direction. Is winning about proving something to someone, or they are focused on improving? Proving or improving? Both can lead to a win, but improving is the longer game.

The best performers are not just winners; they are learners and leaders.

The best performers are not just winners; they are learners and leaders. Their coaching and support team focus on creating learners and leaders in their athletes. They might be current stars, but they are also future stars for life. High performance is a world of learning that can offer both achievement and fulfilment.

Exceptional performers are exceptional people in exceptional systems, but they started like everyone else: a novice with no momentum and no performance system. They had no picture of performance, just an idea of what victory could look like. It is the starting point for every new performer, and the best coaches know how to shift the focus from a win to the process of learning how to win.

Competition

The competitive spirit is essential in high performance; otherwise, the edge and drive are missing. But many feel that success means winning is the whole thing rather than part of it. There is an important balance to find for high performance.

This was starkly evident in training camps when I was an athlete and later as a coach. Without a grounding perspective, winning becomes the main thing. The environment is often one of 'winner takes all'. If you don't win, your chances of staying on the team and keeping the sponsors lessen, and life changes quickly. We say winning isn't everything, but it is often the most visible currency that drives the performance environment.

When over-simplified, it is the puzzle picture that many look for. 'Me on the podium' is a compelling vision, but it doesn't detail the principles of success.

It might seem that winning is the main thing for exceptional performers, but when you look closely, you see a performance picture that is deep, clear and inspiring. We need to build a more profound picture to use each day on the high performance path.

High performers are not just high performers in the finals of the Olympics. They apply high performing behaviours, thoughts, learning and actions each day. Medals are awarded on the day, but won in the months and

Medals are awarded on the day, but won in the months and years before.

years before. And it all started with a decision to be a high performance winner or learner.

It starts early

That decision starts well before the athlete finds a path to high performance. During a family sabbatical in Canada, I coached my son's soccer team of ten-year-olds. After a tournament, a parent from the opposition team was trying to calm the younger brother of one of the players. The four-year-old boy had not played but was disappointed that he did not get an ice-cream along with every player in the tournament after the game. I was about to hand him one when his dad asked me not to. He looked down at his crying son and said, 'There is no ice-cream unless you win. You weren't on the team, so you don't get ice-cream. This is what happens when you don't win'.

The young boy was emotional and confused, and I was stunned. Unfortunately, we often find this anti-high performance language in kids sport environments. Yet when a young athlete arrives into high performance from years within a strengths-based coaching environment, they have deeper confidence and a wider view of what performance means to them

Some athletes can only win the event, while others win both the event and life.

Unlike learning to perform, winning offers no significant or lasting meaning. You can tell the difference – a result is fleeting, but the process it took to get there can be deeply meaningful. It can carry us for the rest of our lives by uncovering parts of ourselves and the people around us that we didn't see before. That is the performance picture we want to be part of. It starts with a decision; to win or learn, to prove or improve.

Have you made the daily decision for higher performance?

Making that decision brings a renewed perspective. The high performer begins to accelerate, unlocking and unblocking potential.

> **Have you made the daily decision for higher performance?**

The deeper game

While winning may happen, it is not the only purpose for high performers – although many people give it centre stage. Wins cloud decisions and make short fixes appear attractive. Conversations fixate on competitive advantage and what others are doing that we need to do as well. Stories abound of poor decision-making and the extremes of abuse, drugs, and cheating – all justified in the name of a must-win approach to high performance.

We are focused on a deeper high performance – reaching high bar victory through focused attention, measured learning and continuous improvement. It is the process and system used to create exceptional performances for Olympic gold and beyond.

In the UK, my first job was working with the head national coaches across twenty sports to create individual professional development programmes. I started with interviews to uncover the main problems the coach was trying to solve. Based on the key problems and gaps in their performance, I would then develop a personal programme tailored to their requirements. One multi-Olympic and world-medal winning rowing coach prioritised a basic cooking class to provide better nutrition for his athletes when on the road. My Director, at the time, was sceptical that a cooking class was meaningful and sophisticated enough for such a skilled coach. He thought perhaps I needed to ask different questions. I inquired further, and the coach confirmed what he needed. A cooking class would improve nutrition and provide an off-the-water coaching opportunity, so we created a cooking class.

Over many interviews across more than twenty sports, I found that the most exceptional coaches were clear about what mattered for performance. Many head coaches saw this programme as an opportunity to attend workshops, find a mentor or learn IT skills. Some brought a menu of requests. But I found that the highest performing coaches had a different, lighter touch. They were most interested in programmes that would benefit and add performance value to the whole team. These were not offline training (at a workshop or classroom) but online and in the field. The commitment they were willing to make to professional development needed to impact the team immediately and not just their coaching.

In 2000, I was asked to create a technology and innovation programme for a new UK sports institute. I had always been interested in sports technology, and the current Board of Directors were motivated to bring a new approach. It was the first structured technology and innovation programme for the British team. Using contacts in Formula One, the military, high-tech industries and academic research, we worked to implement solutions from industry to solve current performance problems in sport.

It took many months of investigation into each sport's preparation and planning to uncover the primary needs and identify a technology or research connection. I found two levels of need – those sports experimenting far and wide looking for opportunities to include in their system. And those with specific known problems that needed solving. One looked to find a problem to fit a solution, and the other looked to solve a problem.

The first group (find the problem) were most open to exploring the many options of potential innovation. From carbon fibre, GPS tracking, instrumented equipment, new training equipment and cryogenics for recovery to 3D video technology, every solution appeared attractive.

Those at the other end of the spectrum (solve the problem) were much tighter on their areas for exploration as they had a deeper awareness of the gaps in their current system. Our conversations revolved around optimising their system and current challenges, and we often achieved performance benefits without adding new technology or innovation.

Those without a clear picture of their system started with the solution – figuring out how to fit the new innovation into their sport. One sport wanted to implement a cryogenic recovery process. When we dug into their performance system, it was clear that their athletes were relatively unfit, and the coaches were not well planned at preparing athletes for the event. These fundamental aspects were more important than cryogenics.

Discussion about the performance system always came first, and if it was not in shape, there was no space to add innovation. In the first few years of the programme, many sports simply focused on optimising and unlocking challenges in their performance system.

As I had discovered through the individual coach interviews, those who were clear on their performance system had a competitive advantage proven by their competition results. Each of us has a performance system that works best for us. The deeper game is uncovering, polishing and applying it.

The performance game

Performance is in all of us. It is the performer communicating and making precisely the right choices to deliver a result in a given moment. Performance is not acting or pretending.

The best performer becomes the performance.

High performance is a learned skill, knowing how to finish and contribute; to bring training and preparation to life. The best performer becomes the performance, and we can see and feel the difference. It is called the peak or flow, and it is in all of us at any time. Not just in the finals at a pinnacle event.

Performance is not only for the athlete. It is a more natural and authentic way to live and perform in our world. Performance is communication and interaction with people and the world. It is you translating your thinking, practice, passion and emotion into words and actions that matter.

Performance is for teachers, parents, leaders, students, artists, athletes, nurses, engineers, meditators. We are all performers unless we have retreated to a cave on our own. If you are reading this book, then finding high performance is the game you have chosen to play.

Systems win the game

Systems win the long game in high performance. What does that mean? Firstly let's define what we mean by systems. You might think of IT systems, or accounting, or marking and testing for students. They are all systems, but in high performance, we refer to the entire performance ecosystem

Systems win the long game in high performance.

around us. These are the interrelated pieces that form you. It involves inter-related processes, networks, people, principles and procedures. The weakest link can impact performance, and interconnections become visible.

For example, one athlete had a car that always broke down. He was often late for training, needed to organise a lift when the racing was out of town, and, as a result, was unreliable. He often spoke of his car as though it was separate from his high performance system. It was his weak link and impacted his training and performance. Together we mapped out his system, and once he saw the impact of each component on his training and preparation (home life, friends, work, transport, and the obvious components of training and recovery), he took immediate action to strengthen the weak link. He couldn't afford a new car, so instead cycled to a team-mate each morning and drove in with him. When we are systems thinkers, we see what matters. Alignment that is off by only a few degrees can immediately impact our world. As James Clear wrote in *Atomic Habits*, 'We don't rise to the level of our goals, we fall to the level of our systems' (Clear, 2018).

This book, Simplify, will help you learn fast, create your system and fine-tune it. If you are unclear about what makes a system, or if you can't identify yours – you will know by the end of this book. When you see what you have, who you are, and what you bring to your game, the missing pieces stand out. It becomes an experiment you fully understand, and the clarity will accelerate you on the high-performance path.

Principles lead the system

You may have heard of the 10,000-hour rule, derived from Anders Ericsson's (Ericsson K. A., 1996) research and popularised by Malcolm Gladwell (Gladwell, 2005). In essence, it describes the volume of experience that is necessary before high performance is possible.

My daughters play music and sing – we perform and busk together – and while watching an interview with the young singer Billie Eilish at her home, they noticed a hand-written sign on her door frame that said 10,000 hours. My daughter asked, '10,000 hours of what?'. And the puzzle begins. What pieces matter most, and how do we put the right pieces together. When we behave and think like a high performer, the performance will always catch up!

The ability to deliver high performance is created through our environment and our attention to our activities. Traditionally, expertise has been judged by the length of experience, reputation and perceived level of knowledge and skill. There is a strong relationship between time at task and knowledge growth, but the relationship between time at task and the quality of performance is weak (Ericsson K. A., 2008). Ericsson discovered that the quality of experience and the deliberateness of practice were the differentiators in people with similar experience but widely varying performance levels.

Quality matters most. Working hard is a distraction to working smart. When you find your system, smarter work improves, and so does performance.

Competitive advantage is about keeping what works and dropping what doesn't.

If you focus on the wrong thing, it doesn't matter how effective or deliberate you are or how many hours you've spent doing it. Competitive advantage is about keeping what works and dropping what doesn't. And this requires deeper thinking to discover and tune your performance system. Most performers are too busy 'doing' to notice the real difference between what's working and what isn't. It is like an addiction to motion over progress. High performers make continuous progress.

Your performance basics

How often do you hear 'Get the basics right'?

But rarer is the statement, 'And the basics for me are...'

The basics are not well-defined because they are personal and contextual to each of us. Your basics are the right things for you, and they are sometimes right in front of you. They are the performer's secret sauce, and uncovering them requires focused attention and experimentation. Finding your basics is the main objective in every 10,000-hour experiment. The faster you find yours, the faster you will accelerate and unlock your potential.

High performance is the basics mastered.

What are your basics for high performance? They won't be characteristics or attributes, so a personality test won't necessarily help you. Nor will they be goals, KPIs or affirmations. They are much bigger, a synthesis of your world, its problems and priorities. High performers make the right decisions more often because their core basics are clear. This is a learned skill that you train and build for yourself.

When you unearth your basics, you have found your superpowers – and they may not be what you think.

What if these basics might be the weaknesses you have been trying so hard to fix and remove? What if these are pointers to untapped strengths? The highest performers have discovered that basics are like compounding interest – find one, and many other system basics will inter-relate.

Finding your basics is a strengths-based approach. It offers freedom from fixing every problem in front of you. There is never enough time to address everything that's wrong, and it will only uncover another problem. Many performers focus on 'find and fix,' where there is plenty of motion but very little progress. The performer's potential is hidden in the distraction of fixing problems.

The busy middle

Those who don't know their basics are busy with motion not progress.

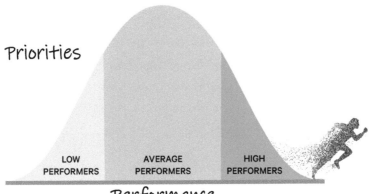

Figure 1: Priorities of high performers

Those who don't know their basics are busy with motion not progress.

I worked with High Performance Sport New Zealand over four Olympic cycles. My work evolved into measuring athlete behaviour and reviewing individual and team performance after the Olympic Games. The focus was to compare performance in the competition with their priorities, behaviours, actions and thinking before the Games. For the past three years, I have continued this momentum of comparing behaviours with performance across many sports and high performers worldwide.

Repeat medallists have the most straightforward explanations of what worked. In simple language, they describe routines that worked and a performance world they found to be clear and effective. High performers were less distracted by aspects they could not control. They survived the experiment where most do not. They exited the 'busy middle' by finding a pattern of behaviour and routines that worked.

The busy middle is where most performers live. There is much to be done to help that group accelerate and reach and experience their potential. Expertise is contextual and if you want to find your competitive advantage, look at your busy middle for pointers on what to drop or move up.

Figure 1 above shows how priorities curve as performers move from a new performer into a low performer, on towards average (meaning they have not reached their own potential) and then to a high performer. The Y-axis indicates the known priorities of high performers, but we could equally change the label to busy-ness, distractions or time wasted. We discover that high performers have fewer distractions and more focus. They live with greater constraints on their attention, recognising what does and doesn't work. This is a learned skill – one rarely taught to emerging performers. Learning to simplify and eliminate distractions maximises potential and performance.

The busy middle keeps busy by wondering what more to add, creating a time-consuming experiment. If we return to the 10,000-piece puzzle with no picture on the box, we find the busy middle spending all their time on a daily hunt for the picture. For sportspeople, it may be the next idea, piece of equipment or technology. Or it may be what the British team is doing with sleep at altitude, or what the Kenyans are doing with a strict carbohydrate diet or what the Australians are doing with mindset training. For you, it may be whatever your competitors, colleagues or neighbours are doing.

It all creates one glaring problem: there is not enough time for the athlete to run all these experiments.

The art of discernment and strategic simplification learned early is an accelerator for the developing performer, leader, coach or manager.

The subtraction solution

Most problems in high performance are additions that need a subtraction solution.

> Most problems in high performance are additions that need a subtraction solution.

Knowledge experts are different from performance experts, as they have a deep understanding of what is around them – they are subject matter experts. In contrast, performance experts have great depth. They are performers and have come to understand what works for them and what they must deliver at the right time. The world has many knowledge experts who do not need to perform. We see them in plenty of industries, relying on the addition of more information, knowledge and skill.

Performance experts (as an individual, team or organisation) turn their orientation to subtraction to deliver what is needed at the right time. Not every expert is an expert performer, the art of reduction is the learned skill of the best.

Not every expert is an expert performer, the art of reduction is the learned skill of the best.

After more than thirty years in high-performance sport, I recognise that the source of most problems is addition (too much of the right or wrong thing), and the answer is subtraction. Knowing what and how to subtract is the competitive advantage utilised by experienced performers and repeat medallists. Deep simplicity requires deeper thinking.

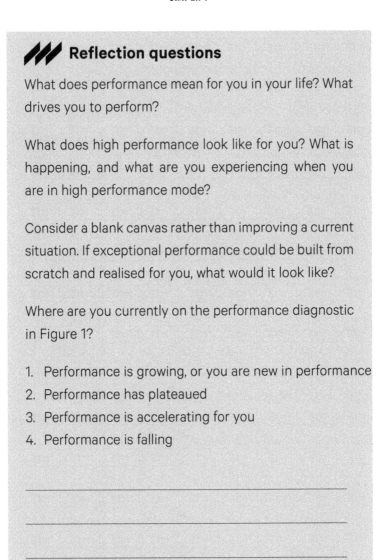

Reflection questions

What does performance mean for you in your life? What drives you to perform?

What does high performance look like for you? What is happening, and what are you experiencing when you are in high performance mode?

Consider a blank canvas rather than improving a current situation. If exceptional performance could be built from scratch and realised for you, what would it look like?

Where are you currently on the performance diagnostic in Figure 1?

1. Performance is growing, or you are new in performance
2. Performance has plateaued
3. Performance is accelerating for you
4. Performance is falling

_____

_____

_____

_____

_____

_____

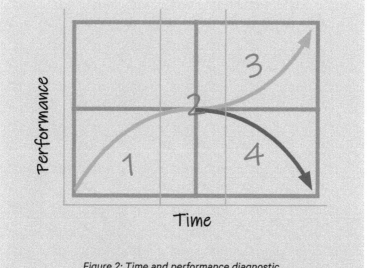

Figure 2: Time and performance diagnostic

Knowing your current level of performance will focus your attention for the remainder of this book.

PART TWO

THE PERFORMER

CHAPTER TWO

TOTAL SELF-AWARENESS

The blue dot on the blue wall

You are like a blue dot on a blue wall. You can't see the system you are in because you are in it. The fish can't see the sea.

You can't see yourself without a mirror, and the performer can't separate from the performance without reflection and a reflector. Many athletes and coaches have a performance life that lacks reflection and contemplation. They put in a lot of hard work and effort and make progress, but reflection is absent or misdirected. I have seen many Olympic athletes (and their coaches) who have no perspective of themselves *and* their system. Following a plan without reflection means they are unaware of their reserve fuel tank.

At the 1988 Seoul Olympics, I met the French national coach and multiple world champion sprint cyclist Daniel Morelon. When coaching, I always sought him out, and we would connect at World Championships and World Cups. He had coached many Olympic and World champions, so I paid attention to everything he shared about performance.

> **The best athletes can see themselves, and the best coaches enable their athlete to do just that.**

I asked Daniel what he regarded as the key factor in high performance. He said that although an exceptional amount of preparation is essential, the best athletes can see themselves, and the best coaches enable their athlete to do just that. When I observed him coaching, I could hear this approach in his questions. There is no learning without self-awareness, and great coaches are masters at building this in their athletes. I have also observed this pattern when measuring athlete and coach behaviour, language and growth over multiple cycles.

Self-aware learners create exceptional performances. It involves knowing who we are and how we are seen. It is the learned ability to observe ourselves and recognise the meaning.

High performers have coaches who act as vital mirrors. Over years of interviewing and analysing Olympic athletes' actions, mental models, and performance, I have never found a repeat medallist who was uncoached. When the athlete has the self-awareness that opens up themselves and their world, then the partnership between the athlete and the right coach can turn into performance magic. A blue dot on a blue wall suddenly stands out in contrast, bringing insights and competitive advantage that only they can see.

Self-awareness for performance

Performers rarely arrive at the start of their performance career optimised in self-awareness – it is learned. Our upbringing and life experiences shape our ability to see. The world can make the growth of self-awareness a challenge through constant busy-ness, shorter attention spans, and communication of 160 characters or fewer. The next priority is tackled before we can think of how we did on the last one, and the reflective process gets crowded in both space and time. We keep moving – sport keeps moving – limiting any time to reflect.

The Social Dilemma is an eye-opening documentary on Netflix (McDavid, 2020). Through interviews with high-ranking technologists inside the biggest tech firms (Google, Apple, Twitter), the documentary explores the rise of social media and the damage it is causing to society by manipulating users. (They point out that 'user' is a term related mostly to addiction and social media.) While the aim of social media is financial gain for the companies and advertisers, nurturing addiction is the method. Addiction is the lowest level of self-awareness, where automatic process and thinking take over. Many of us resonate with this lack of awareness, passing hours swiping the screen. Even when a dead-end is inevitable, the user continues walking toward it – often oblivious and automated. At its extreme, the process becomes so absorbing that it leads to self-destruction like a fatal drug addiction – a treadmill of apparent motion but no progress.

The opposite of self-awareness

When racing for Canada, I was billeted with a family in Philadelphia for a US series. They had two kids, and I raced with the boy. His sister had recently returned home after a year in prison. Under the influence of heroin addiction, she had robbed her family to support her drug habit. She had also been a talented athlete, and the contrast with her brother was evident in their different levels of self-awareness. While he was alive and vibrant, she was an automaton. Drug addiction is an extreme example, but we all have some form of addiction or preoccupation. Recognising it can be a superpower to keep us well and healthy. We are not immune to addiction, but with self-awareness, we can direct our willpower towards good behavioural decisions. You may have heard the saying that 'sport keeps kids out of court'; the key is the commitment to self-learning, self-awareness and self-acceptance.

You may be noticing an additional shift in global self-awareness through fake news and opinions replacing facts. Some news feeds such as BBC and CNN often quote Twitter feeds in their reporting. But where is the fact base in a Twitter feed? The 2016 Oxford Dictionary Word of the Year was 'post-truth', defined as 'relating to or denoting circumstances in which objective facts are less influential in shaping public opinion than emotion and personal belief" (Oxford Languages, 2016). For some, emotion and personal belief are more powerful than facts.

Representing non-facts as facts is another challenge to high performance. A successful cyclist wanted to shift to me as his coach. When asked how he liked to be coached, he said he wanted me to exaggerate his training times to boost his confidence. This is what factless coaching can look like. We chatted for a while, and I explained that a pattern of exaggeration would mean he would never believe me, which could undermine our relationship at a critical time. I also asked if he ever believed his past coach's watch. 'No,' he said, 'I knew he was likely exaggerating.' At that point, we agreed on 'no-camouflage coaching' where we would only speak the truth and facts. He understood that his brain recognised camouflage, and my exaggeration could never truly fool him.

Competition is highly emotive. Public wins and losses measure performance, and a person's current capability is fully exposed to all who watch. Reality and truth are key in responding to this judgment. In an emotional world, facts and evidence are critical for grounding. Deep thinking and patience are turning into a forgotten art and untapped superpowers.

Two tiers

Learning to grow self-awareness is an advantage in every area of life and the critical start line for achieving exceptional performance. The performer **is** the learner. Self-awareness is available to everyone through a process of evaluation and reflection. Without self-awareness, there is no learning and no great performance. We can ask, 'What am I learning about my approach?' and 'What am I learning about myself from this approach?' It and me: the dual perspective and the critical tiers of learning for the high performer. Being self-aware is only half the picture – we need to see the blue box (it) and the blue dot (me).

Without self-awareness, there is no learning and no great performance.

We may not be as self-aware as we think. Harvard Business Review conducted a five-year study of 5,000 participants. Ninety-five per cent of responders believed they were self-aware, but only fifteen per cent passed the self-awareness test and met the self-awareness criteria (Eurich, 2018). Self-awareness is rarer than we expect, and, as this study suggests, we over-estimate our abilities.

Two forms of self-awareness combine to grow exceptional performance. One is internal (how we see ourselves, our thoughts, feelings, strengths and weaknesses, reactions and impact on others), and the other is external (how other people view us). The same Harvard research study found that a high rating in one area did not mean a similar rating in the other. Exceptional performers are highly effective in both areas. We need clarity to see ourselves and our performance and recognise how others see. When the two are combined, the learner is ready to learn.

Accelerating awareness

When self-awareness is seen as a skill to grow rather than just innate talent, we can see and learn from our whole self. True self-awareness is objective. It is asking, **'What** do they see?' not **'Why** do they see me that way?' Why implies something needs to be done, and we can easily side-track down rabbit-holes looking for explanations. These are details we may never understand, and more importantly, may never need to.

> # Awareness is trained first, and decisions come later.

Focusing awareness on current reality does not mean answers; it's just tuning our powers of observation. Real self-awareness combines internal and external observation. Awareness is trained first, and decisions come later.

With deepened self-awareness, we see ourselves in a full-colour palette with both strengths and weaknesses. The first natural impulse is to fix what we don't like. This is the mind-reading trap of 'why' from the novice observer. Here the high performer shows patience. They come to know they are not broken – for high performance, they are complete as they are, and the 'why' question is not important right now. The palette needs to be uncovered to be recognised and maximised. This first stage brings freedom for the future high performer.

No time to fix

There is not enough time to fix everything in the performance picture. A strengths-based approach is an accelerator with only four to eight years of physical capability to prepare and arrive at the peak on time. It empowers the performer to acknowledge the whole palette in front of them.

A successful rowing athlete in the UK was highly anxious, and her support team tried various personal development approaches to fix the problem. The competition was near, and time was running out, so her coach tried a different approach. He repeatedly gave her feedback on how her performance was tracking, and the evidence calmed and lifted her effort, repackaging anxiety into the strength of 'more evidence more often'. The coach reframed the discussion to ask what her anxiety could be identifying that they were missing. 'What need is not being met that we can fill?'

The strengths-based advantage addressed her challenge and kept progress moving. It was a basic that would work only for her and was a key to her performance for the rest of the Olympic cycle. While some anxiety is deeper and perpetual and may need other interventions, this coach recognised the wider view of the athlete in her performance role. Her coach believed the solution could work for her and refocused attention from weakness to strength. Weakness is a pointer to strength on the same spectrum.

Weakness is a pointer to strength on the same spectrum.

Strengths for authenticity

I worked with a world champion cyclist who was very clear about who she was and the advantage that awareness brought her in competition. She would often say, 'I know who I am, and I race better when I don't run and hide from it.' Her message to junior athletes was to 'Stay close, and you won't get hurt,' which I always interpreted as 'Watch what being true can do for you'.

Strength-based awareness is proof that we can work with what we have. Many new performers look at self-awareness as a list builder of things about themselves to fix. It is self-awareness, not self-fix. The best resist digging into meaning and simply acknowledge. How powerful is that? Empowerment is coming to the edge and finding we can pass through, relying on our own ways to work with what we have. When trained to fix weakness and only work on visible strengths, we miss much of the deeper colour of the human palette.

If you are familiar with ACT therapy, you will notice the similarity. ACT is a form of psychotherapy and clinical behavioural analysis that uses acceptance and mindfulness to increase psychological resilience (Harris, 2019).

A professional therapist working with an athlete found the approach we took with self-awareness (acknowledge myself and my performance) synchronised with ACT therapy and accelerated progress. There is a spiral impact to seeing the truth and not always having to solve it, control it, or change it. Just seeing it is all that is needed.

No superheroes

Over thirty years, I have been involved with hundreds of high performers – athletes, support staff (doctors, scientists, psychologists) and leaders. And I can say that the best are fully human and fully themselves, with their limitations reframed as strengths. There is a lightness to their speech, actions and appearance. They are super-achievers but not superheroes with talents from another world. Every performer brings a balanced palette of skills and knowledge to their performance, and they have learned to recognise, acknowledge and capitalise on these. Having had 'fix all weakness' trained out of them, the best prioritise the 'uncover my strengths' approach. It is not easy at the start. Fixing feels like motion but is not always progress. To do this, we must see and work with the true, full picture of ourselves.

> **Had 'fix all weakness' trained out of them, the best prioritise the 'uncover my strengths' approach.**

Performers who were exceptional at their craft had a precise focus on who they were. Their acceptance of imperfections gave them their individuality. All actions and behaviours have a good, or perhaps a confused, intention underneath. This intention points to a strength, but the approach of 'fix what is weak' misses a uniquely personal performance opportunity.

From hundreds of interviews and thousands of analysed interviews and surveys, repeat medallists' levels of reflection was made clear by their language. They openly and distinctly described themselves and their process or system far more clearly than non-medallists. Their language was simpler and more straightforward – not just after the event when the result was achieved or not, but in the months and years in the lead-up to the main event.

The high-performers have a system that works for them. It is the 'blue box' and not always visible to the observer (or initially to the athlete). By examining their language, behaviours and thinking, it is possible to make visible, recognise, and learn from the system they use to create exceptional performances.

You may recognise the alignment here with Carol Dweck's work on fixed and growth mindset (Dweck, 2006). The terms fixed and growth differentiate the learner from the non-learner. Growth mindset is a trait seen in high performance. It refers to the belief that talents, abilities and performance can be developed through effort, good coaching, application and persistence. A fixed mindset is locked in the belief that life is about talents and attributes rather than the possibility of change. High performers know they are made through learning. Learning is the difference maker and accepting that allows us to sculpt, paint and draw with our full self.

The performance will be the best possible with all we have available. The performer learns they are stronger than they know, and this becomes fuel for exceptional performance.

I worked with a young cyclist when I started the National Cycling Centre in Calgary. He was tall and slim, and his parents were athletes. He believed he was meant to be an athlete but was under-performing – waiting for his talent to mature. We discussed that the best athletes are born then made and that while we have no control over our birth, we have great control over how we take on every learning opportunity that presents. We worked on his awareness – not acting on it, just noticing. He recognised that the script in his head was talent-based. Every challenge or poor performance at the training centre triggered a belief that he may not have the talent he needed.

This mental model is exhausting for athletes. We looked at his aims – was he focussed on finding talent or learning skills? As Carol Dweck asked, 'Are we focused on proving or improving?' He noticed that his aim

'Are we focused on proving or improving?'

was to prove he had his parents' talent. It took time to reshape his mental model into learning to improve. I connected him with athletes who had the most vocal 'improving' mental model, and they formed a tight team together to amplify their efforts through supporting each other. He went on to surpass previous expectations and later told me he applied this to his education after he finished competing.

Our colour palette

High performance is daily progress, daily learning and action to close the gap between current performance and potential performance. The high performer is a learner who comes to understand themselves through action, learning and reflection.

At the Seoul Olympics, there was a communal training facility, and a medal-winning US diver was stretching beside me. We spoke about performance and preparation, and I asked what he now knew that he didn't know initially. He said he almost didn't make it as a performance athlete until he accepted who he was and what he brought to the game. He had been obsessed with getting himself 'ready to start' and believed that most athletes who don't make it have the same issue. Many don't feel ready to get started.

We arrive at high performance by uncovering authenticity in ourselves. This is the magic that enables high potential to convert into high performance. Fixing is about creating a new colour palette and, instead, high performers optimise what they have.

Moving from high potential to high performance requires a focus on improving – based on deep thinking and creativity. The performers' authenticity provides the creative strengths to realise their performance potential.

Action is the best approach to discovery in high performance. I've found this to be true in elite athletes – including myself when I was racing. They are often riddled with anxiety and feelings of either being an imposter or not having what it takes. This is far more common than you may imagine. Athletes are measured daily, and a win or loss is usually in public. Any competition win changes their belief system momentarily. This is a strong pointer for future high performers – that belief comes from proof. It does not precede it. Proof can come from the result or, like the anxious rowing athlete, the process. But proof must be there, or the brain will recognise a deeper issue that something is missing and we are pretending.

Action is the best approach to discovery in high performance.

Award-winning composer and filmmaker Robert Fritz investigated the creative process and the power of identity. His pioneering work in structural dynamics and the creative process is discussed in his book *Identity* (Fritz, 2016). Most people have a belief system based on a flawed identity model. Perceptions such as: 'I need to be fit.' 'I need to be the right weight.' 'People think I'm lazy, but when I train, I prove I am not.' 'I'm getting old, but I'm still good at sport, so that proves I am not.' Solving one deep and often unrecognised belief will undoubtedly uncover deeper root cause identity issues. These draw us further into the need to prove our identity wrong, convinced that we need more fixing before we get going and learn to perform.

Proof comes first, but, as Fritz writes, our identity shapes our beliefs leading to a flawed model that we are trying to disprove. It's an unproductive rabbit-hole but points to a reality we need to face to move forward.

I attended several workshops with Robert, and he asked about my family. I have four kids and love doing many activities with them, but I wondered if I was doing too much and whether they may prefer some space. As Robert probed deeper about why I was doing so many activities, my answer arose, 'So I can be a good dad'. He asked, 'Are you a good dad?' to which I replied, 'Yes, I think so, but you'd need to ask the kids'. Robert continued, asking why I felt I was a good dad. My answer circled back to 'because I am doing so many activities with them.'

I could see the link – I had a deep desire to be a good dad to my kids, and because I was not fully confident that I was doing so, I was busy doing lots of activities. At that moment, I realised that some – and maybe many – activities were for me to prove I was a good dad and not always for the experience of being with my kids.

I was shaken and disturbed, but the group was exactly the right place to explore and reflect. The conversation changed my parenting as I reflected on my deeper purpose, which was not to be a good dad but to share experiences with my kids. I lightened up, was more present for the activities we did together and did not pressure them always to be busy doing things with me. It was a parenting game-changer to realise that my mistaken identity was creating an over-compensating situation that was a bit smothering to my kids. I didn't stop doing activities, I just had more presence and quality rather than quantity. I felt the heat was off and no longer needed to prove it. It seemed to vanish once I saw and acknowledged it.

The same happens for performers. When the flawed identity is exposed and acknowledged, deeper options and solutions appear.

Others discover an identity truth. One world and Olympic champion athlete had early-season anxiety challenges (like most athletes) that impacted his preparation. He assured his support team that his anxiety was just a feeling, and he was not concerned about it. He reminded them he was not anxious when he won. He explained that the programme was working, that he should keep training, and the proof would come when he had some wins under his belt. Recognition and action. He knew the wobbles and vulnerability were not telling him about deeper problems. He knew he was a good hockey player, despite not winning at the moment, but the process was working, and he was having a wobble and not hiding it.

I'll gather more proof from training. I believe in proof.

A former Olympic rowing medallist was interviewed after a fourth-place finish. When asked, 'Did you need more belief?', she answered, 'No, I'll gather more proof from training. I believe in proof.'

So, we accept that humans come with identity and belief challenges – and high performers are no exception. In the self-awareness approach, these are recognised and acknowledged but don't need solving. The proof of performance and evidence of progress is a powerful insight when athletes realise they will feel different tomorrow and that fixing this today is not as important as it looks. The solution is today's action and the habit and accumulation of the right action for the longer game.

Belief or reality

Experienced athletes know that their identity and beliefs are not rock-solid all the time and cannot be used to predict the final results. High performers don't 'believe' in every moment. They are humans with regular doubts and anxiety about whether the goal will materialise.

Feelings and identity are entirely human, and high performers need to see them in context. Are they telling me the truth about my potential? Often they reveal a natural negative bias in our thinking – the fear of losing or missing out. Some respond by prioritising 'not losing' (pulling back) over 'learning to perform' (leaning forward). In identity terms, losing proves to others that we are what we believe. It's a perpetual circle.

The break comes when the performer recognises this current reality as normal. It is only now and not forever, and it is guaranteed to change. Actions will create the change, not thinking or ruminating. Words without action are dead. Action changes what we say about ourselves through proof of progress. It is like when a natural disaster occurs, and world leaders say 'our thoughts and prayers are with you'. Depending on your beliefs, those words offer little help to someone with no home and no food. Performers know that action is key, so they get moving and make progress. It's like the Somali saying: 'Pray for water then start walking'.

At the system level, creative action frees up the 'fix me first' mentality. An Olympic medallist in canoeing told me that realising what he believed was not as important as he thought triggered a deep, cognitive change, and he felt freer than ever.

> **At the system level, creative action frees up the 'fix me first' mentality.**

There is no doubt that some aspects are debilitating, and we are aware of so many athletes deep in mental illness who continue to perform. These extreme examples need professional clinical support to unlock and unblock the person. Uncertain performance beliefs are much lighter and in a different league from those associated with mental illness, abuse or neglect. The traumatic end needs professional therapeutic support, but the lighter end can be solved through creative action. There is a time when the performer needs action, not words.

The support team may see a performer struggling with belief and develop an action-for-learning approach that shifts belief systems through proof and evidence of progress. These are the most effective support interventions I have seen.

The performance world is the context, and when taken offline, in a classroom or meeting room, the context is missing. The opportunity to learn and change behaviour has passed. Limited time should pass between awareness, intervention and response. Coaches know this and call it the coaching moment. It is why learning-in-action is both efficient (do it once) and effective (do it in the moment) in accelerating high performers and their systems.

The choice

So we have a choice. The new performer usually feels unready to perform until certain aspects are fixed, but they haven't accumulated enough experience to be performance capable. The Olympic rower knew her anxiety resulted from not enough winning and that it would change with proof. Such facts about the current level of performance and expertise do not need to reflect on their identity (they are not a winner). They are where they are (current reality) aiming to get to a desired future, and as learners, they know they will get there. This is the difference between the exceptional performer and the novice. True confidence is built on proof.

True confidence is built on proof.

Maximising what we have

The high performer focuses on their creative strengths, and the coach and support team are fully aware of the complete picture of the performer. We will come to the coach and support team in later chapters.

My team-mate on a US cycling team clearly had Obsessive-Compulsive Disorder (OCD). The team manager chose to give him a job that met his OCD needs, making him responsible for all our travel, sorting out logistics and packing sheets. As 'CEO-of-packing', nothing went missing or was forgotten. His attitude toward himself changed, seeing that his OCD didn't need fixing but could be offered to the rest of the team as a strength.

High performance is not necessarily a balanced pursuit. I know of many athletes on the spectrum – and for some, that component is a performance strength. With the right coaching and support, high performance gives them an avenue to pursue their dreams utilising abilities that most of society does not recognise. The personal growth that can happen for a performer, no matter their background, can uncover some of the most inspiring stories you will ever hear.

In earlier chapters, we noted that high performance is the basics mastered, which means all of them – good and bad, helpful and not. We either drop it or use it to move forward. High

We either drop it or use it to move forward.

performers don't run away from the truth. They actively uncover, polish and master their own basics that are most meaningful for their world and their objectives.

Strengths-based means we work with what we have. How powerful is that?

Creative strengths help us solve problems and grow self-awareness – once we know how to use them. We live in a world that focuses more on the need to fix weakness, but high performance is at a different end of the performance continuum. It is training, just like any physical sets we have in the gym, but it is training our mental models and mindset.

I have given many talks to high school seniors and asked a group of fifty female students to share their strengths with the person beside them. When I asked what they noticed, they reported that their conversations had changed almost immediately to what they were trying to fix or what seemed disappointing. There was a sense that it was less exposing or boastful than highlighting their strengths. I asked them to consider what brings weakness up, what happens when they live in this weakness and what strength is opposite when they were in their best self.

I walked around to join a few conversations, and one young woman spoke about being an introvert. She explained that she had seen it as a weakness for most of her life, but as co-captain of a school sports team, it became a strength. It gave her the opportunity to step back, observe the team and coach through what she was noticing. She said if she was an extrovert (which she always felt was expected), it would not have given her such strong observation skills. Around the room, they uncovered their own palettes together.

Inspired, a few shared their stories with the group. It provided a deeper insight into how each of the young women was working positively with what they were learning to accept about themselves. And like sticks on fire, the more flaming wood that came together, the higher the flames. By the end, they were a bonfire.

As athletes on the Canadian cycling team, we attended a training camp in Los Angeles, where an American Football psychologist sat us in a circle and ran a similar exercise. It was a powerful experience to acknowledge weakness as strength. We then put the 'weakness' word on our bike to see it when we looked down and behave in the opposite way. We all felt that we had avoided weakness but knew, deep down, that it was there. Putting the word on our bikes meant there was no hiding – it was up to us to find the opposite behaviour. It was a powerful example of concentrating on weakness and choosing to focus on strength in the face of it. We always have a choice. If a weakness exposed a superpower and you could live in that opposite, what would you do differently? This is what the potential for performance feels like.

/// Reflection questions

Seeing your performance system starts with recognising what you bring to it.

- What three strengths and superpowers do you bring to your world?

_____

_____

_____

- What comes most naturally to you? What seems to take the least effort or give you the most pleasure/joy/satisfaction?

_____

_____

_____

- What three weaknesses have you been trying to fix? These may have been work-ons recently or for many years.

_____

_____

_____

- What is the opposite of these weaknesses? If they were resolved, what strengths would they point to? (For instance, perpetual procrastination suggests the power of discernment.)

_____

_____

_____

_____

_____

_____

_____

_____

Complete a timeline (starting from your early years) to identify important events in your life and the meaning they held for you. The lesson may not have appeared to you until years later, and it's likely you are still applying them in your life (use as many pages as necessary).

An example: A coach I worked with had a student who entered a school speech competition at the age of ten. Panicked and embarrassed, he froze and forgot his words. The meaning he carried was that actions hold more power and confidence than words. With that belief, he focused his life on conveying his message through his actions and behaviours.

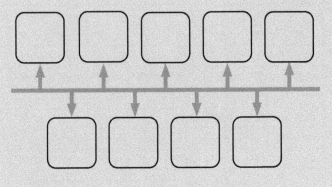

Figure 3: Your lifeline

CHAPTER THREE

VALUES

Values known and lived

High performers operate at a deeper level, on a deeper mission. As we explored in the last chapter, they uncover and bring their whole self to their game. We also know they rely on the clear processes and systems they have discovered work best for them.

Those systems allow them to live and make decisions through values-based performance. They ask, 'How do I bring my values into action?' rather than 'How will this look to others', or 'Can I win this?' Once decisions are clear and aligned with who the performer truly is, every win becomes more meaningful.

A medal is a light goal – the real gold is values. After winning in Rio, an Olympic sailing medallist told me, 'Winning is not the main thing, it is much deeper for me. That is what really helps me win'. Those 'much deeper' elements are the values behind the performer.

> A medal is a light goal – the real gold is values.

We talked earlier about the decision made at the beginning of the high performance journey to learn and improve continuously. That is the personal commitment every performer makes.

Once they have accumulated performance experience and learning, and the picture is coming clear, they face another decision. 'Who do I want to be as a performer?' It is not an identity question where the answer is 'a gold medallist' or a 'repeat medallist'. Or 'the best in this sport' or a 'high paid leader' or a 'high earner'. It is 'Who am I underneath all this? What propels me forward, and what do I choose as my drivers for the future?' Values inform this decision-making, and uncovering and aligning to these give a new high performing superpower.

The discovery

I asked a multi-Olympic gold medallist cyclist how winning so many medals inspired him. He explained, 'I don't do this for winning – that doesn't keep you in the game for long. I am uncovering who I am.' The discovery of the performer becomes the driver in high performance. It is discovery then clear communication, in words and action. The performer uncovers new aspects of themself and communicates that in their preparation and performance.

Flow

Flow in great performances stands out to everyone, whether performing or observing. We don't need a book or a definition to tell us when we are in flow. It is a psychological feeling that arises from the physical experience of alignment between the performer and the performance. The performer is performing, and so is the performance itself; they are happening as one. You may have felt this yourself when absorbed in an activity or a conversation, and the actions or words seem to come from a deeply intuitive place. When aligned within themselves, performers can enter this special zone. Flow comes from accumulated experience and awareness, and can be directly and deliberately achieved through preparation. It cannot be called upon at will, but you can create the conditions to enable flow to occur more often.

Any internal disagreement, battle or misalignment shows in the performance. Values are beneath and inside the best performance. The pre-conditions for flow are embedded in the alignment and communication of values. They are the compass to our decisions, motivations and actions.

> **Values are beneath and inside the best performance.**

Value discovery

Values matter most in our lives, as they offer reasons for our decision-making, even though they are often unrecognised or difficult to articulate. For example, a heated argument over something you can't identify will likely be the result of a compromised value. Just like DNA, everyone has different values. What they are is less important than how they are lived. Common values include belonging, success, friendship, competition, respect, wisdom, but there are hundreds more.

I belong to an international values network called Minessence (Chippendale, 1988). It is an outstanding team begun by Paul Chippendale in Australia in 1988. We are a group of international consultants from all sectors who believe in the power of values and measure, and work with individuals and teams exploring the combined patterns observed across thousands of individuals. We create and coordinate values-centred projects to develop people, organisations and communities, giving collective insights across many industries and countries.

Our individual work is very different, but as a team, we start with values. It is the discovery phase for each person I work with. It brings our lived experience into a 'container' we can make sense of.

Values come first

I spent my entire cycling racing and coaching careers without understanding my values or those of my athletes. Our coaches never explored this with us, so I never did with my athletes. Performance was what mattered most, and we focused our efforts there every day. Certainly, there was respect, honesty and belonging, but personal values and the reasons we were in this game were not made visible to us. So many in sport are unaware of the impact of values on the quality and sustainability of their performance. In hindsight, we felt like anchorless ships in a storm – floating and navigating the environment, but unable to find solid ground.

While racing bikes in Australia, Germany, Russia, France and the UK, I spoke with many coaches from other countries. In some cases, our conversation touched on deeper meaning and values, but at that point, I had not registered the connection to performance. I saw values as a belief and wellness component that was separate from performance. Once I retired as an athlete and began coaching, my perspective began to change as I explored how to uncover the best in others, their teams and their sport.

Values alignment

Later, when I started exploring the creation of personal development programmes for high performance coaches, I could see how they operated and the systems they had created for themselves. By observing their behaviours and listening to the language they used to describe their decision-making, I could hear the value driving their work and their relationships.

When you understand a performer's values, you can also hear the misalignment. Some conversations

When you understand a performer's values, you can also hear the misalignment.

showed that coaches believed they knew what they wanted for professional development, but it did not match their values. One coach wanted to learn techniques for psychological support for her athletes, as she felt she was missing the right language under competition pressure. She had heard of a course with an international psychologist that matched her ambitions. She could describe her intervention, language and the result in the heat of competition. She explained her value of 'team work' as relying on and utilising the expertise of the team around her. We discussed whether she was the right person to attend the course, given her emphasis on developing her team to their full potential. She decided it was better for her lead psychologist to be empowered with this knowledge and bring the new techniques into the team. The decision empowered her and the support team while solving the challenge. She felt this example gave her a new coaching tool to test values in decision-making.

We explored past decisions she had made where she felt the solution was 'paddling upstream' and proved challenging to implement and didn't stick. Those decisions aligned to her values did stick.

Values Polishing

High performance begins as a learning journey where values are uncovered to grow the performance experience. When you see great coaches, repeat medallists and those who consistently perform who are still intensely motivated, you understand that winning is not their only driver. They are winning deeper, uncovering improvements and new understanding every day. They are polishing themselves and their processes daily with a fine cloth. When the performer starts, it feels more like a hammer and a chisel, but the process is what counts. Values are their anchor and keep them performing and polishing their long game.

Most high performers I've interviewed were unaware of their values at the start of their performance journey. But repeat medallists who consistently outperformed others had a clear understanding of their values and those of the team or system they were in. It is part of the natural performance experiment of perpetual growth and improvement. It is the essential anchor in stormy waters and a performance accelerator for the performer and their support team to deeply understand and align with each other.

Energy alignment

Values work helps us optimise and tap into our energy. And energy, not time, is the main currency in high performance. We know a high performer is in a hurry, like a drag race car, and their purpose is to get up to speed as fast as possible and

Energy, not time, is the main currency in high performance.

maintain it to the finish line. Every energy drain on the system (friction, poorly designed components) takes away from the performance. Creating the right system requires a focus on energy.

How much energy do we need? (what standard do we aim for?) How much do we have? (what is our current reality?) What decisions will maximise and leverage that available energy? In this race, the driver is the added complication, with internal motivations, fears and capabilities that need to be integrated with the car.

Alignment saves fuel (time and energy) and creates the freedom to perform. Misalignment creates an uncreative tension that tries to resolve itself. Alignment is natural, and whether we like it or not, it will take energy from performance to resolve itself.

At the World Cup before the 2004 Olympics, I attended a team pursuit training session. This event involves four cyclists travelling four kilometres on a velodrome as a team – one behind the other. I watched as the coaches focused on key aspects; time per lap, how close each athlete was to the inside of the lane (for the shortest distance) and how close each rider was to the rider in front. The shortest distance and being close together in a line are two vital components in team pursuit.

The German coach told me their main work over previous weeks had been alignment. Being directly behind the rider in front reduces the resistance on the following three riders. Team pursuit is an alignment event. The German coach said he could predict the finishing time based on the quality of the alignment between the riders. Physiologically the riders were peaked and ready, but the energy cost would be the decider. Energy alignment can be a predictor of finishing time.

System alignment

For the 2012 London Olympics, I led a group that measured athlete performances. Our task was to compare behaviours and language in the years before the Games, to uncover why medal-capable athletes did not medal and whether there were any predictors. I have continued measuring the impact of misalignment on pinnacle event performance in my current work. Some challenges appear months or even years before. The key message is that misalignment indicators that are not noticed early enough can reappear at the main event. Like a hole in a dam, the pressure starts to build and at maximum pressure (pinnacle event) the hole in the system is exposed. Left unrecognised and unattended, they are ignored and not accepted as potential limiters to the pinnacle event performance.

Misalignment predictors

I continue to explore and support teams to recognise and solve these indicators of misalignment through my current work. Let's look at some of the practical misalignment aspects athletes and coaches identified as preventing medalling at an international event. They point to energy costs preceding an event that directly impact the result at the main event.

1. Arriving with unfinished business. Using our drag race analogy here means new tyres that arrived the night before were fitted but not tested. Or we put a new aerodynamic package on the car but did not run the final tests. Or the driver was ill in the weeks before and therefore not in peak form. The performance system is not aligned to be ready and on time. How often have you been late for a performance (unprepared, misaligned, out of time) and felt it impacted the final result? The highest performer and their system are on time through energy alignment well ahead of time.

2. New ideas and new priorities make the team or performer doubt their approach late in the game. Their core priorities and drivers become uncertain, with new ideas on the table as the event draws near. How often have these entered the discussion late as the performance pressure begins to mount? High performers are clear on what they do and what they don't do in the lead up to the event. When I worked in innovation, many sports came up with highly technical innovations that were 'mission critical' only a few months before the Games. A refocus of energy late in their preparation wobbled the system they had polished and proven in the months leading to the event.

3. Growing resistance to what could not be controlled – a level of micro-problem solving late in the game. While not high leverage problems, these were important. It is natural to pay attention to details and notice more

issues as the pressure builds. When coaching, I would often find my athletes at World Cup events complaining that the warmup did not feel right. Yet, we had deliberately completed the same warmup every day for many months for just this reason. The routine meant they knew that warmup worked perfectly before and would work again today. They were just hyper-aware of their feelings and their level of readiness. We would talk together and remember this was nerves telling them this event mattered, and they were ready. Simply noticing resistance to a proven routine or micro-problems is the magic – it does not need to be acted on. How often have you noticed more about your level of readiness as the event approaches? This is normal for high performers, and those who act on it find the accumulated problem-solving a challenge to their performance.

4. Hoping a performance may surpass what we have seen in training. This is a red flag that something may be missing. If the trajectory has evidence pointing towards a superb finish (this is how world records are uncovered), it is productive to hope that the environment will enable this (wind, approach). Any hope that is counter to the evidence is camouflage that our brain is smart enough to recognise. Hope is an important and valuable flag for coaches and leaders to recognise in their people. How often have you hoped that something would happen when the evidence told you it was highly unlikely? At the Commonwealth Games in Auckland in 1991, my

performance was well under my personal best as I had been ill for weeks and had likely over-trained for a long time. Yet I'd had such hope that my performance would hit the fourth dimension and show us what no one expected – a medal. It did not happen. My performance was exactly as my training times predicted, and I finished in fifth place.

When the performer has proof that the performance is possible, there is productive hope that the performance will materialise. If there is no proof (i.e., the athlete has times that show they are well below their best and have been for years), then hoping to step up is not founded on evidence. If we acknowledge what hope makes visible, we can spot where evidence may be missing and act on this before the event. Energy put into hope and belief is supercharged when it goes first into evidence.

How often have you hoped that something would happen when the evidence told you it was highly unlikely?

5. Communication gaps that existed in the past reappear under pressure (relationship challenges, unspoken resentments and misunderstandings). Like a dam with small holes, the pressure of a big event (the flood) can expose every crack. High performers recognise the

cracks as indicators, and while not currently jeopardising performance, they are high leverage areas that risk performance under pressure. How often has a small communication challenge led to a significant issue that took far more effort to resolve and rebuild later than if it was dealt with on the spot? There is a 'moment of truth' in high performance where the honest conversation is missed. We miss the energy leverage opportunity. Many people I interviewed acknowledged that communication challenges had negatively impacted performance. But they did not think the issue was large enough to reappear and believed it would smooth itself over. That is energy avoidance. Our three choices are to misdirect, avoid or leverage our energy. Leverage is a payoff in the future, and like compounding interest, has more energy in return than we put in. Communication challenges are key energy leverage opportunities.

/// Reflection questions

1. What are your key life values? What is most important to you in life? There are many examples of values lists on the internet. Here is an example from the Minessence Group. https://www.minessence.net/pdfs/values_definitions.pdf

    _____

    _____

    _____

2. Can you point to a time when life or an event had 'flow' to you? Was it a time when everything seemed to fit together, and you were in a peak state without even trying? What events may have prepared you for this state?

    _____

    _____

    _____

3. Revisit the five 'lead-in' indicators on page 42 and identify an important time in your life when you had an unsuccessful outcome. What role did any of these play leading up to that event?

    - Tying up loose ends late
    - Rethinking the main things

- Resisting the flow and uncontrollables
- Hoping where evidence is missing
- Relationship cracks and challenges

4. Now consider a successful outcome and revisit these lead-in indicators. Were they present? How were they dealt with?

_____

_____

_____

_____

CHAPTER FOUR

CONVICTION

Überzeugung

After his Olympic cycling competition, I ran into one of the German gold medallists in the pits. I congratulated him and asked what made the difference in his repeated medal performance. He said he had 'überzeugung,' which translates as conviction. It was entirely visible in the way he and his coach communicated and how the entire team operated. More than internal messaging, his actions proved his conviction to himself and others every day.

Conviction is a deep faith in the performer's ability to learn and deliver well beyond affirmations and positive quotes. Supportive words enhance our outlook and help park our natural negative thinking, but our brains know when they are camouflage for missing evidence.

Camouflage

Confidence and belief are important components in preparation, but they are no substitute for action and practice. The high performer has honed their confidence and belief through evidence and activity, not sitting still reciting positive words. The German medallist's words matched what I heard and saw and the system I began to notice. Conviction permeated his team.

The highest performers behave with conviction in their process. In contrast, novices may rely on a lift from affirmations and belief strategies as they do not yet have convincing evidence or results to prove their capability. Conviction comes with proof.

The highest performers behave with conviction in their process.

With my sons, Ollie and Leo, I watched an interview with Elon Musk after his Space-X rocket boosters returned safely to platforms on earth to prepare for the next flight. What a game-changer for space flight when the rocket is reused rather than disposable. My kids were amazed by the ingenuity and the thinking behind it. Ollie said, 'Wouldn't it be funny if we went to his house and his fridge had Post-It notes saying 'I can do it', or 'You can achieve what you believe'. Elon Musk may well have inspiring messages around his house, but we saw the irony of a deliverer needing light affirmations to keep him going. As Leo said, 'I don't think he needs notes, he just needs to look around.' We figured that Musk sees results that empower his belief. Proof enforces belief.

System confidence is rocket-fuel

A high performer would look at any notes on Musk's fridge and ask, 'What evidence is missing that means he needs affirmations?' A next-level question like this is the world of the high performer, who asks, 'What might this mean and what learning is possible?' Their conviction arises from mental strength that is reinforced and proven through action and evidence. Sure, we can focus our energies on beliefs and affirmations, but when these times appear to the high performer, their focus shifts to beliefs. They ask, 'What more evidence do I need to convince myself?' The realisation is that belief alone is not the reason for lack of confidence. More or deeper beliefs without a clear plan of action is a rabbit hole. It's motion without progress.

More or deeper beliefs without a clear plan of action is a rabbit hole.

The athletes and coaches who use a performance system that works for them have conviction because of the clarity of their actions and evidence that they are truly moving forward. When we add Post-It notes to that level of conviction, we have a mindset supercharged on rocket fuel. Knowing and accepting reality and proving the ability to change it, is a difference-maker for high performers. It is the road to überzeugung.

The innovation hand-brake

I have worked on innovation plans with dozens of sports in the UK and New Zealand. In most cases, I was initially unclear on their current actions and priorities but believed they needed innovation. New and better is always attractive. This is particularly so in sport, where the carbon wheels, GPS, or training equipment design looked to be exactly the solution we were looking for.

I adjusted my work to explore the system they had created. What was their performance context, and how was performance achieved in their world? Basically, what were their core performance basics? If the basics are not clear and in shape, we are adding a new component to a reality we don't yet understand. In my experience, if innovation is delivered before the basics are clear, it acts as a handbrake to high performance.

When we are clear on our performance system (remember the blue box and the blue dot from the last chapter), we see where value can be added and integrated. When the system is misunderstood or unclear, many things can look like a possible solution. Conviction is knowing what to add and what to remove for a performance system we fully understand.

As the innovation conversations continued, the difference between those who knew their system and those who didn't, showed in the ratio of evidence to hope. Hope is very positive – we all need it. But in high performance, hope is a Post-It note. It points to the next question, 'What evidence might we be missing?'

Many coaches hoped that innovation would work for them but had no evidence to support the decision. Hope and conviction do not always align. Nor does looking for magic in new innovations. Conviction is truth, proof and reality. Hope is vital for an optimistic state of mind, but the high performer looking deeper might expect an outcome that the evidence does not support. When the evidence matches the objectives, the performer can expect with confidence. They have conviction. There is no fast road to conviction; it comes from the system and meaning behind doing the work.

> There is no fast road to conviction; it comes from the system and meaning behind doing the work.

Conviction in growth mindset

We referred to the growth and fixed mindset work of Carol Dweck (Dweck, 2006). These terms are well-used in high performance sport, but what do they look like in action, and how is the growth mindset enhanced and lived? Conviction gives power to a growth mindset.

Prove or Improve

The key difference between the mindsets in a high performance context is whether the athlete is there to improve or to prove. A performer who needs to prove themself can have confidence in their ability to perform, but the compass points towards proving something to others. Many performers are in this place in their early years in high performance, and many never leave. When those who win are out to prove something, it eventually catches up with them – not the way to uncover exceptional performance. It is a natural perspective when there is a performance or a 'show' where the audience matters. But when the performer feels they are proving their identity, their belief in themselves, their confidence, and feelings of acceptance, the performance is aligned to making something go away more than bringing something deeper into reality. In Chapter Eleven, we will talk about the power of living in the creative future and how this accelerates the performer's long-term development.

The performer who is focused on improving has a growth mindset.

The language of performers can reveal their mindset in action. One repeat medallist said, 'I am winning, but the challenge needs to grow to keep me motivated' (improve). Another said, 'Life is good when I have the medal – it proves all the doubters wrong.'

A medal can come from either mindset – many performers are motivated by proving to themselves, while others produce victories with constant improvement as their deeper game.

You cannot tell the difference by the result, but the journey has significant contrasts.

Conviction alignment

Every performer finds their natural drivers. When the conviction to improve and achieve is clear and aligned, the individual's growth and performance accelerates. We know conviction comes from evidence that the gap is closing. When combined with meaning, we have a balanced performer playing to win a longer game in life. The proving approach will result in a series of retreat-advance oscillations in preparation and performance. We will explore this further in Chapter Eleven.

We are in a performance system game, but we know that learning-in-action is the real game. When the meaning is clear to the performer, they make better decisions, more often and understand the drivers that lead them. The meaning system behind every high performer is their accelerator. It is an exciting part of the performance journey. It is the system behind the system.

Learning-in-action is the real game.

The high performer's journey

Duff's story, at the beginning of the book, is a high performer's journey. It is the story we are all in; to find ourselves and the performance system we need. Winning sits under the story, but the power is personal growth, the meaning of the adventure, and the metamorphosis of the performer.

Over the years, I have recorded adventures and tracked the learning from many performers whose performance adventure made their activity and thinking visible. When you are on a performance journey, you are in the most meaningful game for life. Let's explore the story further.

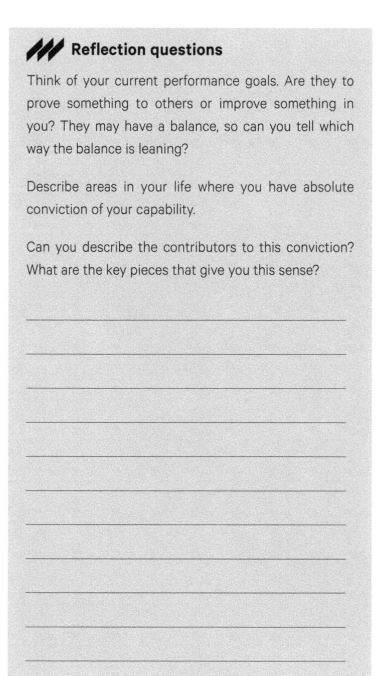

Reflection questions

Think of your current performance goals. Are they to prove something to others or improve something in you? They may have a balance, so can you tell which way the balance is leaning?

Describe areas in your life where you have absolute conviction of your capability.

Can you describe the contributors to this conviction? What are the key pieces that give you this sense?

PART THREE

THE LEARNING TEAM

CHAPTER FIVE

THE TRUTH

Living in reality

When I first moved to England, my job was to create professional development programmes for the UK's national coaches across all sports. I began with interviews to understand their coaching and professional worlds and uncover what professional support would best serve them. I anticipated many specific and highly technical requests, but I heard the complete opposite from the best coaches.

They were clear about what would add value to their athletes and team performance. They were clear on what they brought to their coaching and where their gaps were. In some cases, they wanted to fill the gaps, but in most, they had targeted support staff and a coaching team who filled those gaps. Their team operated as a complementary, gap-filling combination.

One interview stood out, with a national sailing coach with many international medals. She asked that we develop a methodology and listening approach that behaved as a sort of truth meter. She wanted to measure the level of 'rigorous honesty' in conversations across her team. She felt she could solve the important gaps, but only if reality was deliberately represented in all team conversations. Too much effort was going into padding conversations with affirmations and confidence builders, and these made reaching the high water mark a greater challenge. It was an unusual request, but the main message was the value of truth in performance sports conversations.

The approach I took was not to identify untruths but to build the right level of understanding and rapport across her support team so that rigorous honesty became their preferred way of operating. One on the team called it above and below the waterline. We can see clearly above the water, but there is an opaque lens over our eyes below the water. They used this analogy in our conversations, and the response would be, 'I can't see clearly, can you repeat that?' The speaker would replay and try to clarify their message. The directive was to tighten the truth rather than expose untruths.

The story we tell

The human brain makes events fit together to make sense. We

The human brain makes events fit together to make sense.

connect dots even when they don't fit. The truth can unintentionally be buried deep in the story. When the data is incomplete or non-existent, we still extend it to draw general conclusions that fit together. This is how we make sense of the world. That's why witnesses are asked, 'Can you tell us that again?' The listener is looking for inconsistencies to find the truth buried inside. Performance is about the truth – the reality meter that shows where we are. Like a builder measuring a plank before they cut, the tape measure needs to be positioned straight and accurate, or the finish will be off and the target missed.

This predisposition of the human brain to exaggeration is a problem for high performers and even more so for the developing high performer. The performer's puzzle can't be solved without an accurate starting point or repeated measures showing the picture of reality. Stories inform our understanding and our decisions, and an accurate story is key. We need to help our not-always-helpful brains to see the real story in front of us. Not being clear about reality is a limiter to getting to our future quickly.

I have often had athletes come to me from a coach they had previously trained with. This was often due to a change in location or performance, and they were looking for a different approach. I would start with a meeting to understand and share perspectives and to hear their mental models and values. That tells me how they see the world and how they see themselves in it. I still use this approach in one-on-one mentoring or coaching work as a compass calibration point. It's like a ship about to leave the port, testing and calibrating its equipment before departure.

Mental models and values also tell me what drives their decision-making, this is a key insight in a coaching relationship, and we'll explore it in the upcoming chapters. Knowing a person's mental models and values is also a sort of truth meter. We can see when the story may not align and help steer the conversations towards the truth. Few intentionally try to mislead or exaggerate, so in clarifying the story, we both win! The truth is reality, and without it, the gap to our goal is unknown. The truth can hurt, but untruths hurt longer.

The performer's anchor

High performers know reality more clearly than others. The truth is their anchor to reality. As learners, the reality is not so scary. My young son brought a cricket bat and ball home from school, and we played on the front lawn. His efforts missed the ball most times, and his smile was a frown. 'I can't do this; I can't hit the ball'. 'Do you want to learn?' I asked. 'Sure I do,' and a slight smile reappeared. Learning is within our control, and when that mindset is embedded, we have options and can see potential. Camouflaging our resilience with exaggerations, padding, and affirmations is our attempt to make reality look a bit better than it really is.

High performers know reality more clearly than others.

It is important to build up our own truth meter – our check on honesty – it is a training muscle that grows with effort. We are not deliberate untruth tellers, but humans are storytellers and so prone to hyperbole. High performance requires truthful stories, and we all need a bit of help there. It might look like just a slight exaggeration, making the light a bit darker or the dark a bit lighter, but it adds up at the finish. If a Whitbread Round the World sailor is off by a fraction of a degree each morning, they will miss their destination. It is the same in our conversations and our understanding of our current reality.

It reminds me of a joke a coach once told me. A person is driving around looking for a particular street but can't find it. In frustration, they look for someone to ask. A priest is walking by, so they pull over and ask, 'Excuse me, Father, we are looking for High Street. Can you tell us where it is?' 'High Street?' he says. 'Hmm, High Street. Well, if you want to get to High Street, I wouldn't start from here. I'd start from somewhere else.' The exaggeration is somewhere else. We need to start from exactly where we are, and the high performer pays attention to knowing this reality.

High performance is expertise, and both depend on truth. I had the great fortune to meet with the Dreyfus Brothers, Hubert and Stuart, Professors at the University of California, Berkley, in June 2015 and again in 2016. The Dreyfus brothers are the original developers of the Novice to Expert continuum. They had researched fighter pilots, chess players and others to determine the stages involved in becoming experts.

Over lunch, I asked Hubert about the expertise growth I had seen in repeat medallists. There was a very long pause, and I thought perhaps he had not heard the question. His brother said, 'Hubert, Richard asked you a question.' 'I know,' said Hubert, 'but he wants the true answer, not just any answer.'

High performers reflect in action and stay close to the truth, asking, 'What does this mean?' and 'What does this mean to me?'. They have a mirror pointed at themselves and their world – it and me. It is the lens they rely on to gauge current reality, measure if the gap is closing, and align their mirror to their desired future. Reality is the gold standard for the high performer. It is not how clear their vision is but how clear their reality is and how precise their reflective process.

Finding the truth

High performers benefit and rely on the reflection and perspective of experienced observers. They are not alone. They know they can become so deeply involved in tasks, objectives, and thinking that their perspective becomes cloudy. Feedback from coaches and observers clears the air and realigns their focus. Every high performer has a small, tight, experienced and meaningful support team to reflect on the evidence (How are we going?) and share perspectives to determine the best action (What needs deciding?). There are no solo high performers. The truth about reality must be seen and understood by the team, not just the performer.

The best support teams are tight, open and honest – they are the learning team. The best have learned that agreement is not the priority, but understanding the truth is.

There are volumes of research on the characteristics and attributes of high performing teams, but underneath, inclusive thinking, diversity, respect, communication, adaptability, and psychological safety is the truth.

Truth is the principle behind team success.

Truth is the principle behind team success.

Speaking the truth

As discussed in Chapter Four, after the Olympics, we reviewed what happened to athletes who were expected to medal but did not. We explored their understanding of what leads to a non-medal performance. It is a complex system of delay and cause and effect, but aspects that appeared at the big event were spotted weeks and months prior. Unspoken communication was a contributing factor. Aspects withheld, missed opportunities, or camouflaged misrepresented truths turned out to be the most common limiters to performance at the big event. Many in sport work on 'critical conversations', but the underlying requirement in any conversation is the truth. When the truth is a thread showing how a team operates, every conversation is aligned. Critical conversations are necessary when the truth is not aligned and a reset is required. It's best to prepare the groundwork, so these resets are not needed. The highest performers have truth as their core mental model. When the principle and value of truth is a core working guide for teams and individuals, the representation of the truth is not complicated.

Neutral ground

When performance reviews were complete, I would 'talk with the sports' about the post-event findings. Many called the summary 'Switzerland' – a neutral fact-based territory between people that allowed for truthful and critical conversations. The evidence was in front of them. When evidence is missing, the interpretation fills with opinion and intentions, and often appears very personal. Evidence helps to keep conversations honest and clear. The old military line of 'Don't shoot the messenger' applies. The evidence is the messenger, and the team works with the evidence to decide on its future. High performance conversations are about evidence. And when it is repeated and meaningful, the conversations become meaningful.

High performance conversations are about evidence.

As part of the innovation programme in New Zealand, we hired an exceptional mathematician and neuroscientist who had worked with McLaren Racing. He described the saturation of signals that bombard the driver as the key filter in reporting to the engineers. It is the performer's interpretation of the evidence that guides their preparation. Evidence is truth. The post-race debrief involves the lead engineers and strategists facing a screen of data and reviewing the race. The engineers point out vital signals at key stages of the race, while the strategists highlight decisions made that aligned or misaligned with the signals. The driver identifies the true impact of the strategy and engineering on how the car felt and performed. There can be no understanding of the car's performance without insights from the driver who feels the strengths and weaknesses and the collective truth that come together at crucial parts of the race (e.g. grip high but acceleration low). Integrating all the pieces, they must represent the feedback of the race car as an integrated system. Thousands of signals are recorded, but the driver is the primary source of the integrated picture of performance. What is most striking is the awareness and accuracy in their language and observation of themselves and the system they are in.

The presentation of self

Research tells us that some mental models are not helpful in seeing the truth or representing it in conversations. In his leading book on social psychology, *The Presentation of Self in Everyday Life,* author Erving Goffman explained that everyone carries bias into a performance to look a certain way, appear confident, avoid embarrassment and be right. In what is considered one of the most outstanding contributions to social psychology, Goffman discovered a connection between daily life and performance. His analogy is a theatre – a theatre of life. Goffman writes that the best way to understand human action is by seeing people as actors on a 'social stage'. Every actor creates an impression of themselves for the audience and themselves. It is a bias built into human nature but not a high performance accelerator. Imagine a driver debrief or an Olympic review where everyone at the table carried and lived with this performance bias (Goffman, 1959).

I have observed many situations where this is clearly the operational model for a person or team. Once we acknowledge this mental bias is, to some extent, in everyone, we can move to a deeper level in our performance and observation skills. Awareness is the first objective – not actioning change. We simply acknowledge what is happening and what we are noticing. High performers focus on 'the whole truth and nothing but the truth' about themselves and their performance.

Perhaps more than most groups, the athlete's diary is a staple in tracking and observing their growth. The reason for repeated diary entries in sport is not only to monitor progress but also to spot the truth and become aware of patterns and inconsistencies. Acting out social roles is quite demanding, so in addition to the front-stage aspect of our lives, we also have a back-stage area where we can drop the show and be more relaxed, closer to our true selves. We often feel like two people, with one behind the curtain and one in front.

We often feel like two people, with one behind the curtain and one in front.

Reality shows are so popular because we are curious about who is backstage and how different they are on the front stage.

Low performers are all front stage or all backstage. They often forget where they are, and the performance appears somehow disconnected or unauthentic. Or they forget there is a performance to be delivered, and freeze, over-share, apologise or over-think. The flow of high performance is the bridge between the front stage (what we present) and backstage (who we are). The high performer stands right in the middle and delivers both. And this is the place of flow. As the audience, you can tell when you see the truth in the actor or the performer. This is not a magic show or an illusion but the truth in this moment.

The flow of high performance is the bridge between the front stage (what we present) and backstage (who we are).

High performers peel back the layers through learned self-awareness of their true selves and their beliefs. De-layering to get to this point is not our default process, but learning to strategically simplify and reduce creates the magic to unleash high performance.

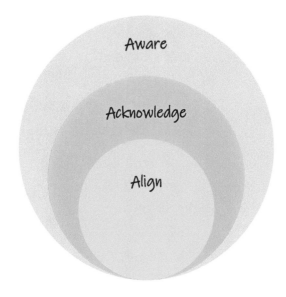

Figure 4: The performance layers

In his behavioural research, Chris Argyris developed Model 1 (theory-in-use: defensive reasoning) and Model 2 (productive reasoning) as either used or promoted in daily conversation. This means we are either walking the talk or merely talking the talk. One aspect of defensive reasoning is the objective of being rational, which involves behaviours such as protecting others from being hurt by withholding information, creating rules to censor information and behaviour or holding private meetings. These are normal communication behaviours, but this protective instinct is counter-productive to performance growth for high performance (Argyris & Schon, 1992).

Argyris' research points to the more helpful productive reasoning (Model 2) where communication is considered a joint approach to learning and growth. This is seen as speaking about directly observable evidence seeking to reduce blindness about evidence, inconsistency and incongruity. Most high performers begin in Model 1, and following awareness and acknowledgment work, begin to operate more often in Model 2.

Behavioural research indicates that we do not naturally point towards the truth in our daily interactions. We have a presentation lens and a protection lens built into us. The high performers on their journey know that this lens needs removing for clear, honest vision. That starts with awareness and moves to action.

/// Reflection questions

Consider an environment you have been in where an agreement was more important than the truth.

Think of examples where you have 'walked your talk'. Your words matched your behaviours.

_____

_____

_____

_____

_____

_____

And consider times where the opposite was true.

What are a few truths about yourself that are known to you and/or others? Explore each quadrant in the model below and consider your top three for each area.

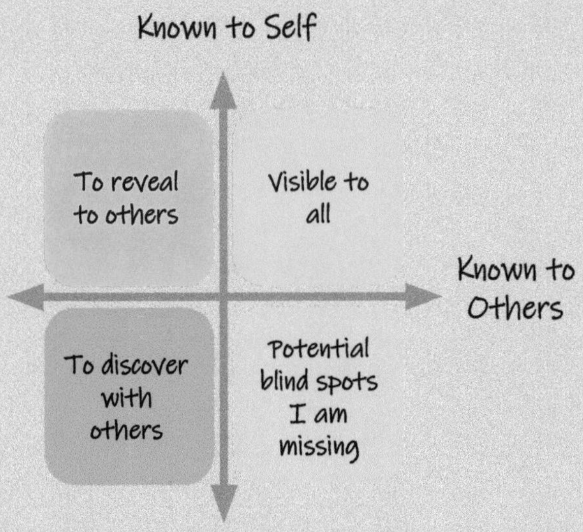

_____

_____

_____

_____

_____

Known to Self

Figure 5: Johari window

CHAPTER SIX

THE ROUTINE OF RIGHT ACTION

Action learning

In high performance, action is either progress or merely motion. Lifting the game requires continuous advancement and improvement. Even minute progress, compounded, creates change. Accumulation of action advances our current reality.

> In high performance, action is either progress or merely motion.

Effective habits

The challenge is to form small habits to reflect on what we are doing and why some actions are meaningful and move us forward. Being busy is full of action, but without reflection, most of us are unclear where motion and advancement lie. Reflection is an action habit. We become attuned to patterns and seeing why actions are happening and what result they are producing. This habit becomes as natural as the action itself.

It all stems from the accumulation of a simple habit of reflection, which is a key high performance habit.

Thinking System 1 and 2

Many excellent books explore reflection and action. Some reflection precedes action (e.g. what do I expect to happen), and some is a review (e.g. what happened compared to what I expected). One of the best books on thinking is *Thinking Fast and Slow* by Daniel Kahneman. He explores why we are not the exemplars of reason that we take ourselves to be. Our actions may be misdirected, and we have biases and uncertainty. According to Kahneman, we have a dual thinking process; two radically different ways to make decisions with two fundamentally different modes of thought. He calls them System 1 and System 2. The first, System 1, is instinctive, associative, and can't be switched off. Kahneman describes this mode as the 'secret author of many of the choices and judgments we make'. In contrast, System 2 is deliberate and requires attention to implement (Kahneman, 2011).

Performance capability can grow through either thinking style, but acceleration and accuracy come from using both. The biggest difference between the two is that System 1 is faster but vulnerable to thinking bias, and System 2 is slow, requires conscious effort and is less vulnerable to thinking biases.

Malcolm Gladwell wrote about System 1 thinking in his book, *Blink* (Gladwell, 2005), describing it as a thin slice of reality, using limited information and narrow experience to decide and act. It works well if we have a trained history of seeing the big picture. When we have built a repertoire of experience and proven we are performance capable, then thinking is more automatic in the moment. This is not reflective thinking, it is 'get the job done' thinking.

Flow in thinking

Mihaly Csikszentmihalyi is the originator of the research behind flow and optimal performance mentioned earlier (Csikszentmihalyi, 1990). While flow involves System 1 when we are deeply in the act, conscious thought (System 2) can make the performance appear more cluttered and calculated. You can see the difference between a novice performer learning their craft and a high performer with more polished skills. It's like a small child learning to ride a bike for the first time. Their thinking is all action, wobbling, adjusting, feet on the pedals, feet off the pedals, rebalancing – all System 2. Then, once they have balance and technique, they evolve more into System 1 (staying upright over a bump, turning sharply), and they are in an early version of flow. System 2 is essential to get to System 1. The more System 2 (reflection) is brought into your preparation, learning routine and thinking, the faster you will accelerate to balancing both systems that will enable you to perform in flow.

Looking up

When walking in your home town, chances are your head is pointed down more often than up. After all, you know where you are and have seen it all before. If you're walking in a new and unfamiliar place, you are likely looking up. A child looks up more than down because things are new and exciting; their brain absorbs new information, consciously or not.

We need a bit of that 'looking up' when things appear familiar and uninteresting. Performance lifts with curiosity, and training in System 2 thinking moves us to a place of interest and novelty. Once we have satisfied System 2 with deep reflective thought, we give System 1 the superpower to take us to a performance level in a new dimension. They are allies that combine to deliver exceptional performance.

We are talking a lot about thinking only to share what may be holding us back. Action wins the long game in high performance. There's an old story of two doors at the Pearly Gates. Both are closed, with a sign pinned to each. There are millions standing in front of one door and none at the other. A new recruit walks to the door with no line and reads the sign 'Heaven', then goes to the other door with its sign, 'Lecture on heaven'. Most of us need to feel ready before taking action, but high performers understand they are more ready than they think and step forward. High performers have learned early to walk through the action door. They

Have learned early to walk through the action door.

are expert at learning-**in**-action and speed past the slower, learning-**then**-action group.

My uncle, Ken Gaye, was a pro cyclist in the UK in the 1950s. When I was a teenager, we talked about training theories. He said, 'When it's time to perform, your theories won't matter. It will depend on how much riding you put in'. Eddy Merckx, the Belgian cycling legend, said, 'Don't buy upgrades, ride upgrades', meaning don't worry about your gear, step forward and put in the work.

The power of lived experience

Action is the great leveller in high performance. Learning from the performer's lived experience is the gold in understanding how and why they chose particular actions. My research into medallists and non-medallists in New Zealand involved mapping actions over sixteen years of historical data. I looked at how each performer, their support teams, coaches and leaders spent their time and what actions they focused on as reported in debriefs and interviews.

See what matters

When we profiled actions compared to performance, the research showed repeat medallists were doing less, talking about less and adding less than the other athletes. The same relationship appeared for their coaches.

The system for repeat medallists is smaller, tighter and more effective. They know which actions matter and why. By looking at their lived experience, we can explore the principles they used to uncover what works best for them. This is the action research that every exceptional performer has mastered. I have continued to test this in my current work with sports leaders, athletes, coaches and business teams. Patterns in the data confirm that the best do less than the rest. What they commit to has more impact and leverage than those who are under-performing.

Reg Revan is the originator of action learning. In the 1950s, he researched the concept based on finding procedural intelligence on the shop floor in factories and offices. He developed a model of 'leadership by walking the floor', meaning we need to know what is happening on the ground. That is where the real action happens and where strategy gets delivered (Revans, 1980). 'Walking the floor' is a metaphor for paying attention to how we vote with our time and attention each day. Great coaches always walk the floor. Great leaders in sport walk the floor. Over the past twenty years, my research and programmes have focused on understanding what is happening on the high performance shop floor. The lived experience, reflections and decision-making of high performers give us principles (rather than theory) to shape our preparation.

Great leaders in sport walk the floor.

The balance

In sport, this translates to the 'Think, Plan, Deliver' model I use as part of a performance diagnostic process. When applied to performers and their system, the model shows where the action is concentrated. Thinking is reflection, hindsight and backward-facing. Planning is forward-facing, and delivery is action in the present moment. The combination forms an action learning process that creates higher performance. We will explore this further in Chapter Ten.

Coaches are heavy in working on the shop floor and performance delivery. They are often reluctant to join a meeting or connect with a review process because their priority is at the track, beside the pool, at the pitch, or in the boat. They are most often focused on the delivery quadrant. Sports offices, however, can be heavy in planning, with full calendars and meeting rooms with people rarely leaving the office. Other sports and leaders focus on reviews, analysis and digging into the evidence. High performing teams and organisations have a collective balance across all three areas. They review the past (think), align with the future (plan), and implement and act (deliver). The performance happens when the past and future are brought clearly into focus. The three then balance, giving an effective past, present and future rhythm with learning, organising and performing, accumulating and collectively lifting each day towards the big event.

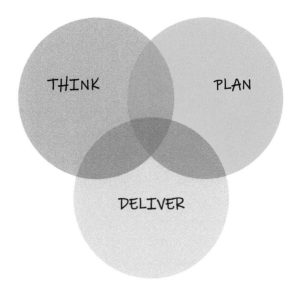

Figure 6: Think, Plan, Deliver model

System building

High performers know how to put the puzzle together. The picture they create comes from connecting the right pieces in the right place to create a performance system. Walking the floor is a key. Looking up is a key. And knowing how we got to this point provides the long-term perspective. In the many talks I give to teams, I usually begin by acknowledging the lineage that brought them to this spot. Although I was not born in New Zealand, I feel the power that communities bring through understanding and recognising their ancestral lineage. In New Zealand, the Māori word for this is whakapapa (genealogy). It is considered a core Māori knowledge (Mātauranga Māori) and is a sharing of identity and history.

Genealogy

We talk about the system game and the importance of an optimised system of performance. It is not the goals you aim for; it is how you plan to achieve these goals. Goals don't separate high performers; systems do.

Goals don't separate high performers; systems do.

Systems are people, processes and how we operate. We rely on historical systems that we have used, removed or adapted – not only the people around us today but also those who have contributed to our growth since childhood. Reviewing an Olympic performance must consider all the effort, thinking and planning across generations contributing to the team. If ignored, we may repeat what isn't worth repeating. Once the lineage is understood, it informs current practice. We stand on the shoulders of many – their best thinking and best actions. There is much valuable insight from walking historical shop floors in your performance domain.

When my kids start a new school year, the teachers often invite students to tell their whakapapa. The process is called a pepeha, which is a way to stand and introduce yourself. The kids put a great deal of time into updating their lineage and looking for what they can share. This is walking the historical shop floor, and we walk forward knowing that much of our performance history is not of our own doing.

Knowable story – reliable system

Many performers never reach their high performance zone because they don't have a system they can rely on. And they often don't have a story behind it that they can articulate. Despite excellent routines of practice, coaching feedback, and clear goals, they never reach their potential. Why? The ladder is often against the wrong wall. And it may have been so for many years. They are putting the wrong pieces in the wrong place and building the wrong chapter in the story. Sometimes the ladder needs a tweak of only a few degrees to hit the magic, the flow. Or maybe there are too many ladders on too many walls. The process on the ladder (deliberate practice, goals, feedback) may be right, but if the eagle is looking the wrong way or is distracted with too many options, having world-class vision and speed doesn't matter. It is motion and not progress.

Looking back over the long history of the growth of performance in high performers, two units of measurement can foretell how this story may end. Energy trumps time and systems create leverage. When energy is flailing and not tightly focused on what matters, time is wasted, and leverage missed. It also happens when systems create action and motion but no progress. The story is still happening, but the happy ending gets pushed further and further into the future.

Energy trumps time and systems create leverage.

The energy to create the right system is the foundation of high performance. Everyone has one system they use and one they are building, but most do not see the bigger picture of the system they are in. High performance is energy management over time management and system building over activity management.

Success habits

Every high performer has found this freedom by uncovering and mastering their system.

In the introduction, I quoted James Clear, and his words are worth repeating: 'You do not rise to the level of your goals, you fall to the level of your systems' (Clear, 2018). Centuries earlier, the Greek poet and soldier Archilochus said, 'We don't rise to the level of our expectations; we fall to the level of our training'. Similarly, the US Navy Seals have several mottos, including, 'Under pressure, you don't rise to the occasion, you sink to the level of your training'.

High performers are system thinkers and system creators in all areas of expertise. What is a system in this context? It is less a collection of things and processes and more a way of thinking.

Take the example of a new athlete who enters the gym and starts a few exercises; upper body, arms, legs. Over time they learn to connect these into a workout with different sets and reps. They continue up the ladder and begin to see their workout as part of a wider system. If they add nutrition, they will have more energy. If they stretch first, they will prepare for an injury-free workout. The athlete explores options that can optimise their preparation. They may add core strength to improve stability or find their recovery is slower than others, so play with different work and rest rates.

From here, they begin to enter the deeper thinking zone of the high performer. Although they may not perform like a high performer yet, they are learning and thinking like one. They begin to see themselves and the process at the same time. Trying out new ways to prepare or optimise their strengths and convert weakness to strengths, they begin to create relationships within their system and uncover links that will accelerate their preparation. This is where the high performer has learned to operate.

Systems thinking is an advantage for sport and life. After I finished coaching, I travelled to Nepal to hike. I happened to sit beside a retired Olympic athlete who was visiting a village where he had spent time. He'd noticed that the huts were smoky because the cooking fires were inside, and there were no chimneys. Returning home, he raised money through business connections in the US and purchased cheap piping to install as chimneys. As he was a good builder, he came and installed the chimneys in every hut. Now, one year later, he was returning to hike and visit the village to see how they were getting on with their new clean air huts. We noticed we had the same return date six weeks later and agreed to meet at check-in.

On the flight home, I asked how the village was doing. His head lowered, and he told me all the chimneys had been removed and were sitting in a rusted heap. Neither he nor the villagers knew that the smoke killed the bugs that ate the roof straw. Once the air was clear and weeks passed, the roofs began to collapse. When we don't understand the system we are in, we can misread what looks like a solution.

When a performer learns to think in systems, they see interconnections, cause and effect, delays, feedback loops and opportunities for improvement. Just like Neo in the movie *The Matrix* (Wachowski, 1999), a new vision for an interconnected world opens up. Low performers are still at the to-do list level of performance preparation and have not clearly linked components into a system. It is the magic pivot point for accelerating performance. The faster we move to the system approach in our preparation, the faster we learn and accelerate. Many get stuck here before they have learned to see the system they are in. It requires a decision to get to the other side – the willingness to do the work and think deeper than before. When we think in systems, our path becomes clearer and brighter.

When we think in systems, our path becomes clearer and brighter.

Marginal Gains

The innovation programme focused partly on marginal gains – the one per cent gains that could compound. Sports have used this approach for many Olympic cycles, and it became widely known and marketed as a competitive advantage through British Cycling and the Sky professional team. You hear stories of innovations and approaches adding a marginal gain and the total resulting in significant programme improvement.

The key backstory to marginal gains is the system to which the gain is connected. What does not make the news is how much background work has been done to understand the system – the blue dot on the blue wall must stand out before a marginal gain is visible in context. For a marginal gain to work, it must not be an added complication. Complex works from the **inside** while complication adds from the **outside**. When the fit is clear, there is immediate integration.

If a broken leg is badly damaged and requires pinning in surgery, there is now a complication (added from the outside) that the system needs to integrate into a complex working model. And like the bone binding and meshing around the pin, the complexity adapts to the added complication. When a marginal gain is added, the system complexity will adapt to the complication and reset. The aim in high performance is a higher performance reset with every

High performers make better decisions more often than low performers.

addition or subtraction. Unless they fully understand the system, they may be entering a long and often unproductive attempt at lifting performance. When the system is understood, the sport has clarity, with every decision seen in the context of the performance system. This is why high performers make better decisions more often than low performers. They know the fit.

The high performer's perspective comes from knowing they are playing a longer interconnected system game. The obvious problem may not be the main one to fix. There are systemic interconnections (do one thing and multiple other things are impacted in future) with delay in cause and effect. The high performer operates with this interconnection/delay lens. Systems are built through addressing the deeper root cause problems, not through solving every problem. When change is made at system level, it runs deeper and longer and targets the real priorities. It operates continually on every decision to optimise the high performing system.

Reflection questions

We vote with our time every day, and how we vote tells us what high performance looks like for us today. As with training, all our days add up to give us our conditioning for performance.

Map your day yesterday, from the time you got up until you went to bed. What did you do, and why did you do it?

Time	Action	Because

Table 1: Mapping your day

If today was a regularly repeated day:

- What habits are missing for you?

_____

_____

_____

- What habits would you keep?

_____

_____

_____

Now consider the Think-Plan-Deliver mode:

- Look further back and consider how past days, weeks and months contributed to the day you had yesterday.
- Look forward and consider what performance adjustments or habits you need to make.

Compare which areas of your day provide leverage (insight and action) with those areas where you are improving efficiency or effectiveness. Divide your day into the tiers below. Which parts of your day did not provide leverage but could have with some adjustment? What adjustment would be needed?

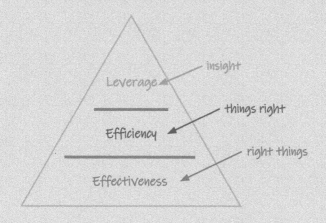

Figure 7: Leverage, efficiency and effectiveness

CHAPTER SEVEN

FLOW SIMPLIFIED

Deciding to simplify

Simplifying is a learned skill of discernment. Systems are built through a combination of adding and subtracting. You will know from your own work that it is much harder to subtract. When the system is unclear, the option to add is far more appealing. The frequency and effectiveness of subtraction is a clear indicator of its importance to the system.

> **When the system is unclear, the option to add is far more appealing.**

Systems gaps

When I moved to the UK to develop a high performance coaching programme, my CEO expected the role would need complex technical skills. He felt my background in performance and engineering and with a PhD was exactly what was needed for conversations with national coaches. The work turned out to require different skills than what my CEO expected.

The best coaches anchored the conversation in the performance system they had created and focused quickly on the most obvious gaps. Sometimes the gap was their own, but often it was elsewhere. I quickly learned that they saw gaps months or years ahead as they explored their development within their performance system.

I focused on system assessment by interviewing coaches, key support staff and leaders to understand the impact of the identified gaps. As one sailing coach said, 'I see you as seeing the system, and even if you don't create a development programme for me, you have already done the job that matters most'. Seeing systems is a performance advantage prioritised by the best coaches, often bringing in outside consultants for a new perspective.

The fit

One coach had six personal development requests that he saw as performance priorities. He wanted to rush them into action before the competitive season started. When we explored these opportunities, it became clear they would complicate his world and overwhelm him, as he didn't fully understand his performance system. We mapped the performance system together, and after a few sessions, he felt he had a vision he could use.

At this point, his development needs changed completely. Through a new lens, he realised that the ability to relate to highly skilled support staff and manage their input and personalities was his highest leverage area. He wanted the support staff connected from the start, travelling his development path with him. The coach recognised he'd had an individual component rather than a system view of his performance world. When his thinking opened up he began to accelerate – and so did those around him. His new performance development requirement demanded rigorous honesty from the conversations within his team.

We found a facilitator through the military who led a conversation framing process that was adopted into their working practice. Every sentence began with 'Here's the truth'. When it was explicit at the start of their conversations, the truth followed. While it felt artificial at first, the team agreed it was hard to begin with the phrase and not tell the whole truth. It was a pointer that I have found helpful in working with teams ever since.

Reducing complications

We are in a world of multiple opportunities and complications, with layers added each day. Adding without reduction makes for a complicated performance life, yet reduction feels like we are missing out. This fundamental principle of 'more is better' is learned early, as advertising shows us how much better life can be with more. We are told that, with one life to live, we should get what we can while we can. Less is not a core of advertising and marketing strategy, and nor is it the natural core message in high performance sport. Look through sport, fitness and health magazines and see everything touted as 'difference makers' for your training routine. There is always a new opportunity, new technology, or something someone else is doing that we need to try.

The simplicity of repetition has stood out in conversations with athletes and coaches, and the better the performance, the simpler and clearer their routine. High performers have mastered the art of reducing the signals that take their attention. Continually adding more just leads to saturation.

We recognise this when we are overwhelmed by a task. There is a sense that we are crowded out with no space to think. The high performers prioritise space to react and respond, which is learned as they prepare for a performance. By reducing the complications of the signals in front of us, we set ourselves up to respond appropriately to whatever comes forward. The performer is not over saturated.

Low or novice performers have a simple world, primarily because they are building their systems and repertoire of experience. There is no need to simplify their preparation because they are not exposed to all the available options. They then move into the performance game and see the opportunities available and what may be missing from their performance. The addition begins and continues to grow – as do the complications in their routine.

Repeat medallists and high performers talked about less, did less and reduced more than others. Further investigation uncovered the overlapping principles behind the systems that guided their routines, approach and thinking. In the years preceding a pinnacle event, we would ask all athletes what they would keep, start and stop for the next event. Although repeat medallists were five per cent of the athlete population, they owned eighty per cent of the stops. They prioritised strategic reduction and simplification over addition to their programmes.

Repeat medallists and high performers talked about less, did less and reduced more than others.

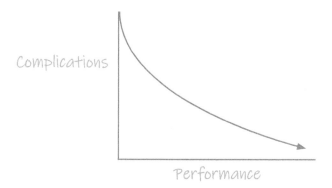

Figure 8: The change in performance through simplifying

Such simplification is not the natural way of the world; we have to create this approach by deliberately deciding to act and learn. We cannot wait for the world to simplify. Athletes, artists and other high performers become skilled at what to bring into their performance at the right time. Learning how to reduce, simplify, prioritise and minimise early in their career is an accelerator to their performance capability.

To simplify means living consciously. Faster is good, but deeper is best. There is often limited depth to our thinking. Einstein said, 'We cannot solve our problems with the same thinking we used when we created them'. The world of more is not the way to achieve faster, lighter or more meaningful performance. As one Olympic coach said before the Rio Olympics, 'It is up to me as a coach to create an uncomplicated environment for my athletes. We are building leaders, and they cannot show their leadership in competition if their mind is full of complications.'

Simplification is the balance of reducing and consciously adding what we believe matters most. It is not **or**, it is **and**. High performers live intentionally, and knowing what to reduce or add is the learned skill of every great performer and coach.

Underwhelming

A conversation stood out with a medal-winning coach before the London Olympics. She said, 'I know we are ready. When the environment is underwhelming, I know we have the main thing in sight, and the team is ready.' She could judge their preparation by observing the environment and their response to it, and she found this the strongest indicator right before the Games.

Coming home

One Olympic medallist told me that he feels at home anywhere in the world because of the stability of his routine. It is the same wherever he goes, and he said it feels like his best friend. The polished routine is always reliable.

> **The polished routine is always reliable.**

Another Olympic rowing world champion explored the edges of his performance routine, feeling confident to add or subtract from his recovery patterns or a new measurement instrument in the boat. Because he had a reliable routine, he said he could always 'row back home', which meant back to the routine that had produced gold medals and world records. He was confident that he could fail fast if a new intervention was not effective.

High performers' environments are surprisingly underwhelming, as the Olympic coach pointed out. There is a glaring difference between those of the best performers and those on their way up. It is not the technology or the talent of the athletes or anything Formula One-like with white tiles and team uniforms. Rather, it is the simplicity of the environment and their ease of access to what is needed. There is a routine, and the team and staff know where they need to be and the next step. The parts fit, the people fit, and the processes work. It takes

> **High performers' environments are surprisingly underwhelming.**

time to create this environment – I call it an ecosystem as it is a growing ecology like a forest or jungle. On the surface, the interactions are invisible, but, over time, you notice that the system is connected and deeply reinforcing.

This is an echo from behavioural psychology and the power of routine and stability in a developing child's life. Anyone who has – or has been – a kid will remember the love of bedtime stories. Research has proven the power of routines (including those stories) to build content, stable and happy young people. A child has periods of rapid development, as does a high performer and both benefit from the same principles.

Many new performers overwhelm themselves with a daunting task and many problems ahead. It is evident in the environment, language and behaviour of lower performers who have not yet discovered their system. Once an experienced leader sees this clearly, they push towards simplifying and aligning the environment.

Their ecosystem is the satellite system surrounding them (home, training space, workspace, living patterns, family patterns, social patterns etc). They see their total environment as an enabler and integrate it into their performance. As we explored in Chapter Four, clarity around values determines the decisions they make about their environment (e.g. family first, nature, hobbies). Environmental stability shows values and clarity in action. There is no standard environment or set of decisions, but to the high performer, it is simplified, minimised and supportive of their whole performance picture. They know performance is a systems game, and their ecosystem is a reflection of their main things. They stay underwhelmed with daily challenges, actively reducing distractions and letting go of what is out of their control.

Context is everything

Stability and the creation of a high performance environment is a contextual problem. That means importing an environment from somewhere else will not work. A Performance Director moved from a medal-winning sport to a non medal-winning sport. His Board and CEO asked if he could bring his previous performance environment into this new sport and his answer was, 'No way. Cut-and-paste does not work for environments. I need to see what we have here – and see it deeply so a new performance environment can emerge'. Emerge, not apply. The best know how to spot the right plants growing in the field and prune and enhance as the growth is happening. It is a dynamic process, and the perspective is the eagle eye of the high performing leader.

Reduction works

Professor Jim Cotter is a great friend of mine and a world expert in endurance physiology from the University of Otago in New Zealand. He felt the warm-up in sport was too long and a waste of time and energy. We often spoke together about optimising a performer's energy. His research proved that a six-minute warmup could target and prepare all our energy systems (aerobic, anaerobic, neuromuscular, etc). But there is a deep mental model in sport that the long warmup matters; it could be to look busy and take our minds off the target for a while.

Stable, simple and repeated is the ideal approach.

My event is sprint cycling, 200-1000m. We would arrive at the venue hours before the event and begin our warmup ninety minutes before the start. Stretching or on the track for a forty-five minute aerobic warmup and then repeated sprints. All for a ten-second event. Our warm-up was busy, and staff preparing gears and wheels was normal. I often see busy at the pool, track, pitch, or circuit, but it is a mental model that the best have moved past. Stable, simple and repeated is the ideal approach. Deciphering what is essential is a combination of reading the evidence and observing what is emerging. High performance environments enhance and simplify routines and behaviours in the current environment, so that all energy is moving and progressing toward the performance objective.

Best principles

Best **practice** does not succeed all the time because context leads. Best **principles** are what work in high performance. When guided by best principles, we can base our decisions on that clear compass. What are your best principles for high performance?

When I was a new performer in racing, my best principle was weight. The weight of my bike was the limiter, so my decisions were about lightening my sprint bike. I even took a drill to all my expensive components – including my seat post. (Don't ever drill out your seat post. I had to replace it after the first race when it snapped, and I was left sitting on the broken end for a brief moment.) I also filled my tyres with helium. My principle led my thinking.

Another athlete I knew believed leg strength was the key and decided this was the best principle for him. He spent too much time in the gym, used electro stimulation and grew in size and strength, but this did not translate into his performance. His principle was not the best one. We can hear these principles in how people communicate and in their actions. In new performers, these emerge based on who they meet and what they read, and it is important to listen and see these in action so a re-steer can happen. The guiding principle of 'simple and stable' works. To create simplicity and stability, the performer, coach and leader need to know what is working and what needs to go.

SIMPLIFY

/// Reflection questions

Each day is training. We don't need to look further than a single day to see how we create high performance for the future.

Describe a recent day when your world seemed complicated. What complications stand out to you?

_____

_____

Consider a day when the world seemed simpler. What, if anything, did you do to create this?

_____

_____

How can you simplify a complicated day?

_____

_____

_____

High performance is contextual. We are a mix of some high, many average, and some low performance behaviours.

What are your top three in each category?

_____

_____

Which behaviours get most of your attention?

_____

_____

How are these impacting your overall performance?

_____

_____

_____

_____

Priorities

LOW
PERFORMERS

AVERAGE
PERFORMERS

HIGH
PERFORMERS

Performance

PART FOUR

THE OPTIMISED SYSTEM

CHAPTER EIGHT

THE HIGH BAR

Desired future

When you know the height of the bar, you know how high to jump. And more importantly, the gap between the bar (future) and the ground (reality) are visible.

Having worked with more than thirty sports on performance reviews and strategies, I am always surprised by how few know the height of the bar. They may have a goal of Olympic gold, but that is an aspiration. You cannot plan or measure an aspiration until the event is finished. The desired future must have a number and a picture that you can see.

> The desired future must have a number and a picture that you can see.

Know the routines

When coaching sprint cyclists, we would analyse the competitors before we arrived at the competition. We knew the gear they were likely to use (there is only one gear in velodrome racing, so you had to choose the right gear for the day's race). We would know where they look when they race to uncover blind spots. We knew how they preferred to win and where their strategic gaps were.

We also understood their primary training process and routines, their coach's approach to performance, and their team environment. We made sure to understand not only the physical location where we were racing (weather, heat, humidity, pollution, wind, velodrome structure, local food and transport) but also the competition environment (distance to the food hall, types of food, transport type and length of journey, even how hard the beds may be). This is standard procedure in Olympic performance. The more you know about the environment you are walking into, the better your training and preparation for the event. We knew the future scenario and adapted our preparation to close the gap in our preparation every day.

Knowing the environment

I led the acclimatisation programme for twenty New Zealand sports preparing for the Beijing Olympics. We convened three years before the Games and met each quarter to discuss the collective strategic plans to ensure the athletes were ready for Beijing's heat, humidity and pollution. We would bring all the groups together and elaborate on our strategic plans.

We sent scientists to Beijing to measure the heat, humidity and pollution and compare our data with what the Chinese government was publishing. We had GPS sensors in the sea to measure tide, sea temperature and wind direction for sailing. We had pollution meters on top of buildings and worked with an environmental group in New Zealand to analyse and uncover patterns in the Beijing environment. Every athlete was tested for exercise-induced asthma, and the medical team prescribed medication for those over the line.

Our approach to acclimatisation was a standard reference point around which each sport would develop its own strategy. We knew the exact pattern for years before – even including potential storms in the Gobi Desert – so we felt strongly prepared for a worst-case situation. At the end of the acclimatisation process, sports told us that the thorough investigation into scenarios and principles helped them arrive with confidence and a routine that they could reuse for other competitions in challenging environments. Unless you know the bar you're trying to reach, you can't have a meaningful strategy that deals with the current reality.

Know who is watching

Knowing the bar is vital outside of sport too. I have two daughters, who are both musicians. Gracie sings and plays the guitar, and Emily-Rose sings, plays the ukulele and writes songs. Three of Emily-Rose's songs have won national awards in New Zealand. They both enjoy the occasional competition, and we enter several national competitions, including the 'Gold Guitar'. In their first year in the junior class, they got through to the final. The grand final performance moves competitors from small venues to performing for several thousand spectators, with a big screen, lights, a band and professional staging.

After making the final, they became curious about being better prepared for the big event and potentially winning the competition. We spoke to judges about the main things (the bar) that would be observed. It turned out that stage presence (movement and freedom) was important. As Gracie and Emily-Rose had not rehearsed how to move, hold the mic or make eye contact with the audience, this changed their rehearsals. Now they knew what was assessed and needed to bring a new presence to their performance. They also brought this to their singing to match the flow and movement on the stage. They both made the junior final, and Gracie won the Junior event overall.

The puzzle of performance becomes much simpler when the bar is visible each day.

We are not musically competitive; we love playing together at home and for family and neighbours, but the experiment of 'How high do I need to reach?' changed their approach to rehearsals and preparation. They could see the bar, and this moved their practice and performance into a clear line of sight. The puzzle of performance becomes much simpler when the bar is visible each day.

Knowing the competitors

Many Olympic teams and countries track the performance of global sporting events using data captured by a company called Gracenote (Nielsen, 2021). They hold data on every major sporting event, athlete and performance. The ability to analyse the global picture of sport performance and know precisely the competitors' current best times and rate of progress means that the physical and the competitive environments are known.

For months before the event, we tracked the progress of every athlete in every Olympic sport to determine the standard needed and the likelihood of winning a gold medal. In most Olympic systems throughout the world, the analyst's job is to understand the overall competitive environment and performance level before any competition. Even in judged events, video content on YouTube and Vimeo show so many competitors' performances and tricks that it is hard not to be aware of world standards. The Winter Olympic team, for instance, has clear insights into the types of tricks on a snowboard, how many rotations in the air and how high off the edge of the half-pipe (the venue where the athletes perform spins and tricks) will win a gold medal. The athlete's job is to reach or even surpass that standard.

Seeing the gap

High performers who see the finish in detail and know the associated numbers regard their actions differently. They have context and evidence to commit to what matters and reduce their activities in areas that do not impact performance.

The thinking gap

High performers have learned to think differently about their training. They are progressing on a deliberate path that they fully understand, towards a desired future they can see. They are also intentional in paying attention to the impact of their training. Repeating the same tasks over and over without question is why many performers stay stuck.

> **Repeating the same tasks over and over without question is why many performers stay stuck.**

These challenges are no different from those we face each day in business and life. Exceptional work in organisational systems theory has been effective in sport. Daniel Kim (Kim D. H., 1994) developed a theory and an approach in practice to move organisations from reactive problem-solving into generative learning. The focus on a learning organisation and transforming performers into learners is key to reaching a high bar.

Kim's Levels of Perspective model considers five levels from which to uncover the system we are in (Kim D. H., 1999). He points out that the further we shift from seeing only specific events toward understanding what influences them, the more leverage we have. Professor Kim was influenced by, and partnered with, Peter Senge who was instrumental in the research behind systems thinking (Senge, 1997).

Systems thinking was a game-changer for how business and performers saw their world. The framework gave clarity to a path that previously appeared cluttered. When we understand that all systems follow common principles, we see how these reveal patterns, interconnections, and the delay in cause and effect. It is like a crystal ball showing where our current path may lead based on behaviour principles that apply across the system.

Performers with a systems thinking framework can think more clearly, connect the dots of the system they are in, and learn and influence while in action. By exploring how we think and act and the leverage in daily life, the performer can see how specific well-focused actions can produce significant lasting change. The performance lens is tuned towards leverage and impact and the exceptional performer's system begins to open up. Whether or not the outward results have caught up yet, their system has now been enabled.

The event in front of us

Let's explore the levels of perspective and how they may apply in our lives. What we see in front of us is called the event. It may be a single instance such as driving to work, eating dinner, patting the dog, listening to the news, practising the unicycle or training in the gym. They are apparent when we plan or review our day. Most people live at this level. High performers live there too, but their thinking takes more of a helicopter view. When we live solely at this ground level, the world is full of either problems or non-problems. The human brain is designed to focus on problems – that is simply survival instinct. Solving them at this level is reactive and never-ending, and, unfortunately, it is where I see most stalled performers.

The patterns that appear

When activities repeat, you may or may not notice patterns. Repeated events speak to us when we become aware of them.

Repeated events speak to us when we become aware of them.

For instance, you may discover that you hit all the red traffic lights when you drive a particular route to work, meaning you are always ten minutes late. Patterns get our attention when we are conscious of our actions and reflecting on the meaning behind them.

This is the first question; what patterns am I noticing, and what are they telling me? Remember that high performers are always conscious of their actions. For most of us, patterns are automatic and remain hidden or unrecognised. New performers who live consciously at the patterns level pay closer attention to the past so they can plan, anticipate issues and events, and adapt their behaviours to close the gap to their future.

The future picture is clear to the high performer, and they are committed to continuous improvement and deepening their thinking system. Operating here brings a new perspective. We have a new lens starting to appear – it's like an eagle's eye, able to see further, clearer and in more colour than humans. Did you know an eagle has the best vision of all living species? They can see eight times further than humans, meaning they can see a mouse three kilometres away. They can also shift focus to zoom in on their prey. They can see a wider range of colours, so prey stands out from the environment. Their ability to see the UV spectrum tells them where the mouse has last been via its body heat and waste trail. In effect, they can see history (Miller, 2008). Systems thinking gives the performer their own eagle eye – a look at history through the lens of interconnections and cause and effect. There are always systems behind the events that contribute to the patterns in our life. The causal relationship between systems and patterns enables you to see structures. A whole new world opens up, and you won't want to go back.

Systems behind the events

Patterns tell us there's a system hidden inside. Books such as *Blink* (Gladwell, 2005) and *Thinking, Fast and Slow* (Kahneman, 2011) provide evidence of our quick decision-making brains. But high performance requires deeper thinking as we aim to uncover the profound simplicity behind what matters most to our performance. This involves another deeper reflection frame, and we pause to ask: 'What is causing this pattern?' Here, performers start to develop their exceptional performance system by uncovering the maximum value and deciding what to deliver at the right time.

In Olympic reviews, we would collect data on team members in the years preceding the Games to show performance patterns (competition and training results) and behaviours (debriefs and interview results) from each athlete, the support staff, leaders, and the team. Compared across time, athletes and sports uncovered patterns in performance and preparation that helped us understand the Olympic results. The systems and structures were the main investigative area and always provided deeper insights. By seeing and improving the system, we create leverage. Long-lasting improvement and accelerated performance come by focusing on leverage areas rather than efficiencies (doing things right) or effectiveness (doing the right things). Leverage is about doing the right things in the right way every time.

> **By seeing and improving the system, we create leverage.**

Leverage

Once we understand the system, we can see improvements needed, what is working so well that it needs to be kept and protected, and what we can drop. Leverage includes delegating, connecting other people's skills and talents more effectively – including our own.

That's evident in the story of one team that, with the Olympics approaching, was becoming more like two. Criticism of others and behaviours and language showed a growing 'them and us' culture within the team. This was both alarming and surprising to the coach, who had a world-class background in building team cohesion.

As we explored further, there was an apparent systemic reason for the growing divide. The selection criteria for the final team was not published to the deadline. The leaders wanted to keep the team together for as long as possible but did not realise their message was confusing. Missing the selection publication deadline meant rumours spread, and there were backroom discussions of who would and would not make the team. Team members felt the rules were no longer clear, and their behaviour matched this lack of clarity.

All Olympic athletes know and accept that there is a selection process. But despite good intentions, ambiguity was pulling the team apart. Until we investigated, no one noticed the underlying patterns in the months leading up to the Games. Initially, the support team thought a particular athlete was negatively influencing the team. Then leadership thought the head coach no longer had the team's backing because of past world cup performance. Once the pattern was exposed and explored, the underlying reason was spotted, tested with the team and confirmed. Earlier, a potential 'army of good intent' would have kicked into action to solve all the wrong problems, thus further dividing the team. Sport often has the expertise in-house to solve the right problem, but performance suffers if it turns out to be the wrong problem.

The thinking behind the system

We worked with the team to uncover how this selection challenge had arisen. System changes come directly from thinking changes. According to the Levels of Perspective model, we think first then create systems to match our thinking. A better approach is to find the system then look for the thinking patterns that created it. This is the place of deeper leverage.

In the example above, once the sport saw the system, they could investigate the thinking that produced it. It turned out the new leadership felt keeping the competitive edge to the last minute would be a performance advantage, but had not made this message visible to the team. Historically, the sport had always spoken about selection early in the training phase, selected as early as possible, and never missed a publication deadline. Every athlete had known what was required and when the decision would be made, but they were unprepared for what leadership saw as a slight change to the process, and the impact was larger than expected.

When uncovering the thinking, we discovered that the senior coach and senior leader had disagreed about athlete selection early in the year. The senior leader was exercising his power over the coach by adjusting the selection process. Once understood, we could bring the two together, show them evidence of how their disagreement played out for the team and demonstrate the overall impact on team performance. Times were slightly slower, and the language and behaviour indicated that distrust and lack of clarity were unsettling previously strong relationships.

A further meeting was held to resolve the deeper challenge between the two roles and communicate a new message to the team. With the selection criteria reset, the team went on to produce a medal at the Rio Games.

Values lead thinking

Once the sport discovered the divergent thinking between the two key roles, they explored the final level that informs thinking. We discussed values in Chapter Four, and this is where thinking patterns are formed. Collectively they revisited their team values and how these were playing out in their behaviours. They discovered that the leadership group did not trust each other. This was very sensitive, but the facilitator managed to bring the whole picture into the open. A 'no trust and low truth' environment in the leadership team kept important conversations unsaid. The selection data was only a symptom of a divide in the leadership team, and the athletes' behaviour began to mirror what was happening. Systems are interconnected; what happens at the end has shown its face

High performers not only practice deliberately, they think deliberately.

at the start. No plant grows without roots. The event triggered a cascade of thinking, system building, and behaviour patterns opposite to the team's normal behaviour.

Mental representations

Newcomers who adopt high performance thinking are already high performers.

High performers not only **practice** deliberately, they **think** deliberately. Visible patterns of activity and thinking provide leverage for performance. An athlete interviewed after the Rio Olympics said, 'Every practice is physical and mental – how much faster can I move and how much deeper can I reflect on this.'

The performer who sees the system transforms into a high performer as a thinker and reflector. Newcomers who adopt high performance thinking are already high performers. Their competition performances will catch up.

/// Reflective questions

What is your most crucial performance goal?

Describe in detail the environment where you will achieve this goal. Do this through your senses – what do you see, hear, smell, feel, taste?

_____

_____

_____

How would you behave in this scenario when you are in flow and optimal? Consider your actions, your words and your state of mind. What is the desired future?

_____

_____

_____

What would be missing in your preparation if this performance was today? Consider your current reality.

_____

_____

_____

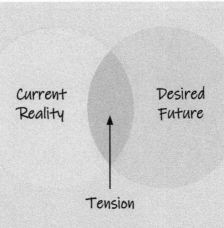

Figure 9: The tension between current reality and desired
future, based on the work of Robert Fritz (Fritz, 1989).

The overlap between your current reality and desired
future is the performance tension to be resolved. What
would be your first action to contribute to success and
begin to resolve this tension? Keep mapping ways to
resolve this tension.

_____

_____

_____

_____

_____

_____

CHAPTER NINE

THE EVIDENCE

Lean learning

Before the London Olympics in 2012, I was asked to redevelop the performance review model in New Zealand. It was essentially unchanged since the 2000 Sydney Games and relatively standard across Olympic performance review for previous Games and most countries. It was a large, all-hands-on-deck undertaking after the Olympics were over. In some cases, the data collection was outsourced to a group such as IPSOS. Occasionally the full review was led by an external consultant or a law firm.

In-house matters

The first step was to ensure all the historical performance data was captured and available. Previous reviews are rarely revisited, but they often uncover patterns that are only appearing today. Like radio signals from space, there can be a long lag time in performance and paying attention to patterns from past events can lead to immediate competitive insights for the next event.

In a post-event review, the win or loss has already happened, emotion is high, and energy low. There were concerns among the team that fingers would be pointed, and there was a perceived agenda to the interview process. These mental models affected the honesty of the data. Seeing the post-event review in the context of the pre-event review removed the emotion and revealed underlying patterns of action and thinking. These were checked during an interview for accuracy and deepened investigation. Overall, the questions were repeated before and after the event to unlock differences and permit comparison across groups.

Reviews are often crowded with many interesting questions, but the focus is on uncovering all possible details of what happened and why. This is a deep rabbit hole that draws attention away from the next event. The next event is what matters now; the one we are reviewing is over. We only need enough information to inform decisions for the next event. Most reviews miss this simple concept and become a balloon of questions and interviews. More data has a corresponding reduced impact on the next event.

We only need enough information to inform decisions for the next event.

The questions matter

To improve the performance review process, we first pulled together all the performance review data we could find since the 2000 Olympics in Sydney. That covered more than 3,000 athletes, support staff, coaches, leaders and managers. When counting, we found 2,000 questions were asked over sixteen years. Many were similar, with slightly different wording, which reduced the count to 700 unique questions. The most important question we expected to see was 'What do we do for the next event?' But that rarely appeared in any interview. The expert with the lived experience spent at least an hour with the interviewer, but every question focused on the past. They were almost never asked about the next event. The interviewer was expected to figure that out and pull this together in their recommendations.

Lived experience

Based on their extraordinary work, I contacted Hubert and Stuart Dreyfus. I've described meeting them earlier in the book. They had developed a model of skill acquisition that proposed that learners pass through five distinct stages: novice, competence, proficiency, expertise and mastery (Dreyfus & Dreyfus, 1980). We wanted to use this model as we were interested in the growth of performance and what was contributing most and least to the performance growth of all roles (athletes, coaches, support staff and leaders).

I wrote to the Dreyfus brothers, and as they were both passionate about sport and deep learners, they agreed to meet at UC Berkeley. I also contacted their former PhD student, Professor Patricia Benner, who had applied the

Dreyfus novice to expert model in interviews with nurses. Her work explored the novice to expert continuum across nursing careers, informing nurse education around the world. It was incredible meeting at Professor Benner's house with the Dreyfus brothers and Patricia's husband, Richard Benner, Associate Dean at the Haas Business School.

That meeting completely changed the performance review process and my perspective on the value of the novice to expert model. I was fascinated with Professor Benner's research methodology using phenomenological inquiry. The lived experience of the performer and their support is the key. While most methodologies focus analysis between qualitative and quantitative research, a phenomenological study explores what people experience and focuses on their experience of an event and the meaning they give to that event. This is the main perspective in sports performance. What is their experience, and what have they learned? What do we do next? As phenomenology has a strong foundation in philosophy from thinkers such as Heidegger, Sartre and Merleau-Ponty, Professor Benner's living room discussions were a deeply insightful philosophical exposition of why people behave the way they do. I had found my mentor team to improve learning in high performance sport.

Previews matter more

The first stage in adjusting the review model was to change the name to a 'preview' model. I met with professional soccer, rugby, baseball and American football teams and explored review processes from the military, air-traffic control and surgery. In each of these sectors, the preview process was standard practice. By uncovering the meaning of performers' experiences, informed decisions could be made that led to increased higher performance at the next event.

Before and after

From successful reviews in other industries, we noted a series of questions to uncover the current reality and compare it to the desired future. We then refined them to a repeatable set of six questions:

To uncover current reality:

1. What is going well and contributing to my performance?
2. What has not been going well and is detracting from my performance?
3. What worries me currently about my performance?

To explore what is required for the future:

1. What do we keep to improve or maintain performance?
2. What do we start doing?
3. What do we need to stop doing?

This question tool is easy to remember and effective in simplifying how you pay attention to your actions, results and next steps.

High performers need the truth and actions; they cannot create their future without it. Like a ship's compass, the direction needs repeated checking. We do this with athletes every day to gauge improvement. There is not just one measurement before the World Championships. Small, frequent and repeated samples are necessary to uncover patterns that matter.

Your own backyard

When we see our path, we uncover our answers and basics. New performers spend more time looking over the fence than investigating their own backyard. In contrast, high performers know their personal detail before observing the practices of others. The context and reference points are clear: if we don't know what we do and why we do it, everything else will look like a possible option. Performers who are tracking in the right direction get clear on their process before adding and innovating.

Innovation starts with defining what is currently done. If you can't define it, you can't see it, and if you can't measure it, you can't see it. We use a research approach (repeated sampling and reflection) to decrease random experimentation. High performers are not afraid of hard work; in fact, it attracts them. But without repeated sampling, it can camouflage the wrong strategy and wrong actions. Most are only a few per cent away from finding their rhythm and sweet spot. Measurement is the only way to make adjustments in action.

Accumulation

As evidence accumulates, we start to grow intelligence and understanding about what we are doing each day. Remember, attention and energy is our fuel and how we spend it is typically a mystery to novice performers or wheel spinners. The advancing high performer has a conscious understanding of their world and what actions they give their energy to. At this stage, we begin with a log of activities without looking for reasons. Weekly check-ins reveal what the patterns are telling us.

This is an evidence-based experiment that delivers results faster and builds a deeper sense of who we are and the process we are creating for ourselves. It is an exercise in self-awareness and performance process building. The best performers know themselves better than the competition. Many performers who do not master the high level of delivery are missing this. They have explored many options but missed the opportunity to uncover what is working or needs adjustment within themselves and their process.

> The best performers know themselves better than the competition.

The diary on rocket fuel

With a regular routine of tracking and reflecting, you come to a place of simplicity – and that requires deep thinking.

It is no coincidence that an athlete's diary is a standard tool in sport. Every performing athlete who is repeatedly measured and tracked reflects on progress and polishes areas through deliberate practice and aligning priorities.

My cycling teammate kept his diary close beside him – often in his hand when not on the bike. He would record multiple entries every day; what was happening, how it went and what needed to happen. He had developed this rhythm and stayed with it for years. I found it unusual and inspiring. At a race in the US, he was interviewed with his diary in hand. The interviewer asked if that was his 'black book'– the one with all the secrets. He answered, 'This is more than a black book. It is rocket fuel.' Once we have the data we need, it is rocket fuel for decision-making.

In prioritising truth and evidence for growth, high performers need a record of actions and learning. Novice performers are yet to have convincing evidence of their capability, and a record can help them recognise where there is progress and where there is only motion.

We need a simple, repeatable method to track actions, decisions and learning. When an approach is too complicated, time-consuming or has too many documents or apps to make it work, we have lost the point. An easy and memorable tool will prove what we are doing and what we need to do. It is rhythm and reflection that counts most.

Acting on evidence

To the high performer, evidence is the decision-making difference-maker. Am I moving closer or further away from the big goal? As we saw in the last chapter, the perspective of the high performer is wider. Even the way they see their day fits into a system measured by the evidence of energy. Where are they spending their energy, and is it creating progress and leverage? Energy management and attention management win the long game. You'll need to be a gold medallist with your energy well before you win a gold medal on the field.

> **Energy management and attention management win the long game.**

Energy management beats time management

You probably know of the urgent and useful quadrants, made famous by the late Dr Stephen Covey (Covey, 1989). This model originated with US President Dwight D. Eisenhower (Bast, 2016). Before becoming President, he served as a general in the United States Army during World War II and became NATO's supreme commander. His military command meant he had to constantly make tough decisions, which led him to create the Eisenhower principle to prioritise time. For high performance sport, time management is less critical than energy management. Performance requires action, and the quality of our action matters.

There is a lot of 'busy' in sport preparation, and the urgent-important quadrants provide a view of the collective actions and how they may be affecting results. Time management can be addictive. It is like moving chairs around, with full calendars of meetings and full days of movement, driving, talking and phone scrolling. Time passes, taking our energy with it. The best performers are clear about where they place their energy and attention, and how long they hold their energy in one place.

Busy is not progress

We are in a deeper, longer game and how busy we look or feel is unimportant. Are you getting the right result? Where is your primary focus? Working smarter means energy. Working harder means time. When the time and energy are balanced, acceleration builds. In interviews with repeat medallists versus non-medallists, we explored language use and James Pennebaker's work on the power of language and pronouns (Pennebaker, 2011). Repeat medallists used the word 'smarter' more often than 'harder' and the pronoun 'I' more than 'they'. The non-medallists talked more about working harder, doing more and looking for reasons for their performance outside of their responsibility. The medallists worked smarter and focused on taking personal responsibility for their actions and change.

> **Working smarter means energy. Working harder means time.**

High performers in the energy game see the bigger picture and know their energy is leverage, and momentum begins to infiltrate into other aspects of life. Knowing what to do first separates the best performers from the rest. They consistently know the next best step and make better decisions more often. Their perspective gives them a clear application of energy and attention.

Energy quadrants

As discussed earlier in this chapter, the most effective decision-making questions involved what to keep, start and stop. To prioritise energy in these areas, we put them into a quadrant model to identify what is currently contributing to performance and what could be improved or dropped for better performance.

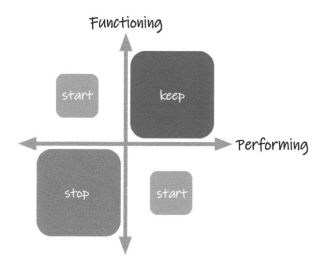

Figure 10: Keep, start, stop quadrants

When we map where we are spending our energy, we can see what is important to us in our day. Looking deeper and mapping our daily/weekly/monthly priorities on this quadrant grid, we find some are high contributors to performance and highly functioning on their own. For example, a performance analyst may have software for post-game video analysis. The software has a high performance contribution value, but often it requires hardware changes and a software upgrade, and the analyst works more on getting the software to function than on delivering performance value to the coaches. The aim is to spend most of our energy on high functioning and high performance contributing components.

High performers aim to stay in the top right quadrant, applying their energy to what is useful to performance and reducing effort and energy on activity that is not.

I have used this 'keep, start and stop' model when preparing for three Olympic Games. A simple action mapping exercise that I work through in leadership and team coaching is identifying the main energy fields and optimising them. What is often surprising is the amount of activity in the bottom left quadrant, where activity is not working or contributing to performance, but has not been dropped and continues to take energy. If you've ever been involved in something that you know doesn't work, but is hard to give up, then you'll understand this category.

Dividing actions this way enables us to see which activities are **functioning** as they are (i.e. Do we need to put energy into fixing or refining them? Or do they do what they are supposed to do?). Which areas are **useful** to performance? (i.e. Do they contribute to performance improvement?).

The areas to start refining or start delegating are shown in the top left and bottom right corners with the smaller labels 'start'. These may provide opportunity if shifted to the top right. They are either functioning or performing but currently not both. This is where areas of opportunity may present themselves. It's important to map the energy required to move these items to the top right. It may not be worth the time or effort when balanced against what to keep and stop, which have immediate performance value.

In working with people and teams to map their quadrants, there is usually great surprise about where energy is spent, followed by the recognition that energy alignment can immediately impact performance. The map of where we spend time is a visual description of what we believe is high performance. When we map and reflect on these behaviours, we notice patterns for improvement that were often hidden.

Perspective

When the goal is important, do what the best athletes do: pay attention with short check-ins to make quick adjustments on the fly. We make decisions at every step based on the best information we have. We step forward with no plan or strategy.

We make decisions at every step based on the best information we have.

When measuring forwards and backwards, using quick snapshots to focus, we see reality – where there is progress, and we accelerate. The combination of action learning and evidence tracking is the equivalent of having a clear hindsight (past) and foresight (future) lens to see the picture from both directions. When learning-in-action is added, we gain reflection in the present moment, creating a lens like a hologram, with an image from all sides.

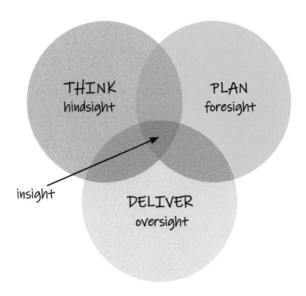

Figure 11: Insight at the intersection of thinking, planning and performance

Reflection in balance

Low performers are often out of balance, focusing on one or two areas, so performance falls or plateaus. All high performers are balanced in three areas that combine to produce results: Think. Plan. Perform.

Thinking, in this model, is reflection on the past, or hindsight. Are our actions creating progress or just motion?

All high performers are balanced in three areas that combine to produce results: Think. Plan. Perform.

Planning is the predictive edge we need for creating the future – the foresight that can close the gap. Performing requires oversight of both; it is the interaction of energy and insight. Insight is seeing the picture simultaneously from the front, from behind and in action. When the performance system is made clear, decision-making becomes more accurate.

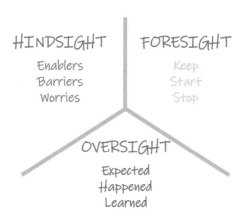

HINDSIGHT
Enablers
Barriers
Worries

FORESIGHT
Keep
Start
Stop

OVERSIGHT
Expected
Happened
Learned

Figure 12: Prompting questions

Think: hindsight

Our brains are belief engines, not truth engines, and patterns of thinking and behaviour expose unhelpful activities and assumptions. That is critical leverage for performance acceleration. While post-event performance reviews are common in sport, they are often too late, too infrequent and too slow. Repetitive simple processes work best to capture vital evidence from the past and make decisions for the next event. Knowing what worked (enablers), what did not (barriers), and what looked to be the deeper unresolved problems (worries) are crucial to understanding.

> **Our brains are belief engines, not truth engines.**

Plan: foresight

In sports, looking forward typically happens after a big event, when plans begin to form for the next one. In many sports, the high-performance plan is their entire foresight picture. However, the real performance picture is dynamic, not fixed, and requires a future-focused, foresight approach with an edge.

Performance decisions are made in the moment, with no immediate plan or strategy. Reflecting on what action is needed to move forward (keep, start, stop) will make visible the evidence for these decisions and uncover patterns in thinking and behaviour that help align the compass.

Perform: oversight

High performance is know-how in action. It requires exceptional oversight of what is most important to deliver what is needed at the right time. Every action reveals a high-performance intention. It shows what a performer believes high performance is in any given instant. Learning-in-action means informing while performing – a learned high-performance skill.

For example, having had experience with hundreds of performance plans, three questions deliver effective in-action evidence.

- What did I expect?
- What happened?
- What did I learn?

Sports with weak thinking and planning processes have the most significant gap between what they expect and what happens. They are more often surprised by unanticipated events.

High performers who have balance across think, plan, and perform are more aligned and make more accurate decisions.

Insight

High performance requires deep thinking and simplicity. While some ask the wrong questions or too many of the right questions, simple insight systems work best. The key is gathering just enough evidence to inform decisions – and

Victory is within the system you are in!

no more. This means decluttering the review process to make it more meaningful, forward-facing and easy to implement. High performers pick the shortest path to the right evidence to make decisions that matter.

No time or learning is wasted. Gold-medal capable systems are more important for the real game than the medal. The evidence and learning system in many sports is over-complicated and infrequent, hiding untapped competitive advantage. Victory is within the system you are in!

/// Reflective questions

Consider your performance goal and map:

- What are the three main enablers that contribute to your performance?

  _____

  _____

  _____

- What are the three main barriers detracting from your performance?

  _____

  _____

  _____

- What worries do you have about your ability to achieve this performance?

  _____

  _____

  _____

Next, consider each response and its level of functionality and performance. For instance, you may find your training facility is an enabler but is too far away with an enormous commute to train properly twice per day. It would be a high performing enabler (great venue) but not a high functioning enabler (too far away). Or perhaps your outstanding physiotherapist is a high functioning component, but if she is so busy that you can only see her once a week, then she becomes a low performing component.

Map each of your earlier responses into this performance matrix which spans maximum functionality and maximum performance.

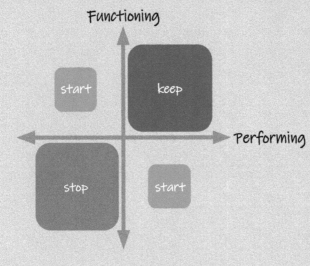

Figure 13: Performance matrix

CHAPTER TEN

THE CREATIVE FUTURE

Fixing vs creating

Interviews with athletes after an event are very insightful. One such interview was with Olympic and World medallist and world record holder, New Zealand rower Mahé Drysdale. At the Beijing Olympics, he was ill but still competed. He had been targeting a gold medal but finished in bronze position. A reporter asked him how he would take better care of his health next time, and he replied, 'I can't always control my health, but I can train harder next time, so I can win when I am sick'.

You can hear where Mahé is focused: not on fixing a situation but creating a new future. Fixing is motion, but creation is progress. Creation is the difference between performance and exceptional performance. The high performer is not free of things that need fixing – they are simply free of giving them their attention. They point their attention and action to what matters and create their future. We can see that no great leader is built purely from winning.

> **Fixing is motion, but creation is progress.**

High performers act deeper, with the awareness to face reality and lead the change to their desired future.

Future and reality

This is an insight into the perspective of the exceptional performer. They live in reality and point their attention to a future they know they can create. Being in the creative process is the difference between those performers and the rest. Fixing the current reality (arrive healthy) or creating the future (win when I am sick) shows the creative performer's direction. They move forward by focusing their energy on where the leverage is. If they can arrive healthy and win when they are sick, they have twice the power. Focusing on how to fix circumstances is a fixed mindset. It can create motion, but we know progress is more important.

In coordinating the Acclimatisation group for the Beijing Olympics, we could see the difference between those who prioritised fixing and those focused on creating. We explored what we called the Bermuda Triangle of heat, humidity and pollution. Many who were already familiar with competing in hot, humid and polluted climates felt this process was overly detailed and took attention away from the main things. Their perspective was on current reality, and they saw no need to do anything different. However, the approach was a creative process where we would lift the awareness of the teams who had never experienced the Bermuda Triangle effect and combine the creative thinking in the group to uncover opportunities and competitive advantage for the future. This was not about fixing reality; it was creating an entirely new approach to adaptation that could be used across sports.

Perspective shift

The perspective shift accelerated our work together. From my experience, many in sport are consumed with the day-to-day busy, trying to manage a giant list of actions. The creative future is where performance gains are made, competitive advantage is found, and the performance system becomes interconnected and optimised. Across so many sports and roles, the Acclimatisation group achieved this through alignment to create a new future.

The lift up from the many logistics of acclimatisation to answering the question 'how acclimatised do we want every athlete to be?' is a system question. It helped keep the group aligned to the Olympic dates and the state of each athlete.

Alignment in perspective

Sport can carry a lot of history and experience in its collective intelligence, and those are conditions for misalignment. Highly skilled people all trying to solve problems can be the usual way of working in many sports, even those who are winning medals. But they are not optimised for sustained exceptional performance until perspective aligns across the system. Without that (fixing versus creating), there is short-sightedness in the daily work. Only the leader and head coach carry a longer-term higher-level vision and think beyond the day or the week.

Many performers and those in performance sport are busy fixing the present, and until they notice the difference, they will never find their performance alignment.

When you hear an orchestra warming up, it sounds like chaos. I remember taking my young son to a philharmonic concert, and we walked in as they were tuning their instruments. My son said, 'Dad. They can't play – did you already pay for this?'

An orchestra warming up is an accelerated version of the creative process used by high performers. First, they explore their tools and skills (tune their instrument, clear the mouthpiece). Then they listen to those players closest and connect their tuning to the tight circle around them. The musician's perspective widens when they hear other instruments and align their tuning, rhythm and melody. The orchestra begins to synthesise, and although the tuning sounds chaotic, it seems to have a connection just before the conductor taps the lectern for silence. They gather themselves, ready their instruments, and create the symphony together on the conductor's lead. Fixing is like perpetually tuning, while creation is the orchestra aligned and performing. I don't believe you can have a 'fixing' focus and become an exceptional performer.

Fixed mindset and fixing mindset

As we discussed in Chapter Three, a fixed or growth mindset is a difference-maker in sport. Your mindset can either lead action or follow it, but either way, it must be connected to impact your reality and influence others. From my work comparing medallists and non-medallists, this mindset-action appears as either fixing or creating. Are you a learner or focused on talent only? Are you trying to make present problems go away, or are you creating a bigger picture focused on high-leverage problems? These are the real issues that need addressing for higher performance.

Rising up

High performers advance to their desired future. When it is time to perform, they work with what they have. They create rather than fix. Low performers rise up and lower their future, rise up and lower again and again. High performers have cleared the way. They accept reality (limitations, lack of control) and move forward to create the future. Low performers pull back to try and fix reality, then move on and return to fix something else. It's a perpetual spinning wheel.

Oscillation

High performers keep the bar high, while lesser performers may reduce their desired future to meet current reality. Remember the cyclist who

You cannot fool your brain; it recognises camouflage instantly.

asked me to inflate his times to boost his confidence? By lowering the bar, he hoped to appear closer to his future than he really was. That is not keeping the imaginary bar high, it feels like progress, but we know the difference. You cannot fool your brain; it recognises camouflage instantly.

Science has explored the idea that 'one lie leads to another'. The camouflage creates an oscillation in what we say as opposed to what we believe we should do. A study published in *Nature Neuroscience* (Garrett, 2016) showed a relationship between brain activity and a lie. Our response to a lie is an emotional response in the amygdala. But the study found that over time, the emotional response in the amygdala reduces with each lie. We can learn to live with camouflage. There is self-benefit or self-protection at the heart of what is happening, and the emotional response is because it does not fit the way we want to view ourselves, which is as an honest person. The study found that to compensate, we can influence brain activity to 'reduce the pain'. The pain is the incongruence between our actions and what is important to us. Living consciously is the way to congruence.

The exceptional performer is deeply aligned and congruent in what they say and what they do.

Creation requires constant attention to break or avoid the cycle of incongruence. The performer never intends this tension, but the deeper picture of congruence is a deeply held value in all of us. The exceptional performer is deeply aligned and congruent in what they say and what they do. When we stop thinking about our actions in practice, we can become complacent and automatic. When we are incongruent for too long, our brain activity can help us to live with it. Our thinking has lightened, and our performance will do the same.

The creative edge

Creation takes a philosophy of adaptation and transformation. Exceptional performers have a creative edge; the best in the game – those who have won all there is to win – talk of their hunger to improve past performances. The outward medal, trophy or prize still counts, but the picture of performance is a much deeper and even more challenging experiment. As an Olympic gold medal winning coach recently told me, 'My curiosity is to uncover and sustain the most complete performance system in the world'. Her efforts are to explore, create and redefine the performance problem. And her athletes are aligned to the quest. Despite winning often and consistently, they are polishing the system even deeper for a future that is unlike their current reality.

The identity of the performer

If performers are consumed with fixing, other aspects may be at work, related to a deep level of identity that is performance-dependent. As Robert Fritz discovered, when identity is too tightly meshed with performance, there is an oscillation. Fritz's research with exceptional performers in art and business showed fluctuation between fixing and creating (Fritz, 2016). There will be periodic advancement but often a pulling back. In my experience in performance assessment, athlete learning and performance reviews, an oscillation is often unnoticed, but once pointed out, the pattern can appear visible over months and years. Some days performance times are progressing, and on others, they are not. Our team is aligned, and then it is not. When the data provides a helicopter view of these patterns, it can be evident that the oscillations are frequent and have been going on for years, unrecognised and unnoticed.

We all have labels that we are either trying to prove or disprove.

Fritz wrote, 'What you think of yourself is irrelevant in the creative process.' How freeing that is for perpetual fixers. Fritz's work also explored the destructive impact of identity stereotypes, racial prejudices and obesity labels when we hold them as part of who we are. We all have labels that we are either trying to prove or disprove. Knowing what it is helps us acknowledge and move forward without oscillation. Fritz went on to say that 'When you get the attention off yourself and onto the outcomes you want to create...you can experience new joy and involvement, and life can move from an ongoing struggle to a true creative process.'

That creative process is the world of high performers.

Making it happen

Actors embody the story of the character they play. Athletes embody the physical and tactical high performer they have become. Industry specialists embody the years of know-how they have accumulated through on-the-job experience. We see what people know and how well they know it by how they perform. They are communicating.

Performance is more art than science. All performance is the art of communication. When we see a performer in flow (smooth, clear, deep, effective, natural performance), we connect at a deep level. We are in the performance with them, and they are feeling, not thinking, their way through it. They subconsciously embody instant creativity. The experience is mesmerising, and we remember these performances long after they end. The audience is deeply part of it, with a connection to creative performance intelligence. When we experience this as an audience, in dance, a tennis match, a leader's speech, or an inspirational book, we know we are at one with something profound.

They are creating in front of us, and we are in their creation with them.

The performer's preparation and learning brought them and us to this spot. They have prepared for just this, and that preparation has allowed them to uncover something deeply meaningful and often spiritual. They are creating in front of us, and we are in their creation with them. This potential is in all of us and is a learned skill.

Itzhak Perlman is a virtuoso violinist who walks on stage in braces as he was struck down with polio as a child. The Houston Chronicle reported on an event during a concert at Carnegie Hall in New York. Perlman was only a few bars into the piece when there was a loud snap as a string on his violin broke. Everyone thought he would have to attach his braces and leave the stage, but he didn't. Instead, he closed his eyes, nodded to the conductor and played with passion and power, unlike anything the audience had heard before. Of course, it is impossible to play a symphonic work with three strings, but Perlman continued, playing music more beautiful than ever before. When the applause of the crowd subsided, he was called on to say a few words. He said, 'Our job is to make music with what remains. In life, everyone is on centre stage, and much lies broken in every one of us. But we need to play even if we have only three strings. We are capable of creating music with what we have left that is more beautiful than we ever imagined.'

That is performance. When we approach performance as the creative process, we bring both flow and depth to life. That is the real game we are in. And the one worth winning.

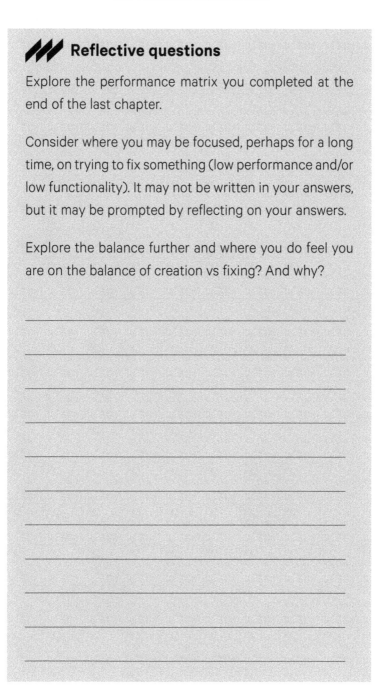

Reflective questions

Explore the performance matrix you completed at the end of the last chapter.

Consider where you may be focused, perhaps for a long time, on trying to fix something (low performance and/or low functionality). It may not be written in your answers, but it may be prompted by reflecting on your answers.

Explore the balance further and where you do feel you are on the balance of creation vs fixing? And why?

_____

_____

_____

_____

_____

_____

_____

_____

_____

_____

Everyone is partly fixing, but the high performers are creating more. How can you shift the balance towards creating and pulling yourself to your future rather than pushing yourself away from your past?

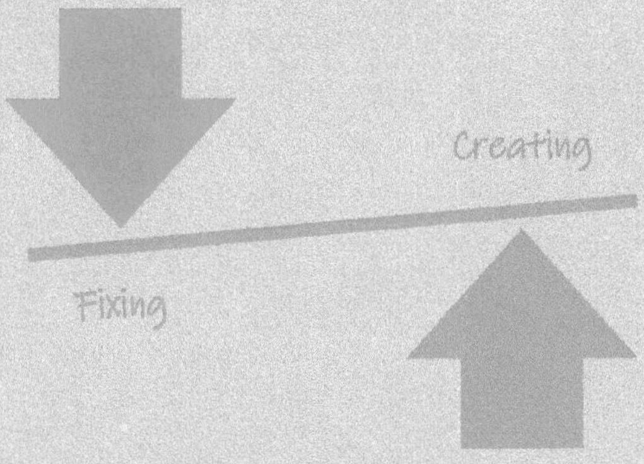

_____

_____

_____

_____

_____

_____

_____

_____

Figure 14: Creating or fixing

Further discussion questions

How aware are you of yourself and the system you are in? Can you see both concurrently?

Is your team focused on rigorous honesty or agreement? How can you shift ever closer to the truth?

Do you fully understand what it takes to win? Do you have a clear picture of the environment where your performance will take place (use your five senses)?

Do you collect the evidence that matters, and what questions are most important to repeat?

Do you have a proven routine that you can rely on to prepare for performance?

What do you value most in life? How do these connect you to your higher performance?

Have you ever experienced conviction about your capability? What were the reasons for your sense of conviction?

Do you and your team have flow in the daily preparation for performance, a flow that comes from the rhythm of good habits and routines?

Are you creating your future or fixing your present? Do you feel you are pulling your future closer or pushing your past farther away?

THE PERFORMER'S DASHBOARD

We have travelled far. Let's put the picture together.

We know that exceptional performance is in us all, and through these chapters, we've explored a pathway to high performance. We lifted self-awareness through a reflective performance process, seeing performance as communication. We recognised and uncovered blind spots in our outlook and approach to performance. We examined our actions and perceptions of ourselves and our systems through a lens of truth. We adopted an action mindset. We recognised the value of systems thinking and understanding the systems we function in – knowing that we will flourish in the right system. We understand there are interconnections, cause and effect, and delay that are unseen or unnoticed. As a high performer we face reality and decide each day to learn and improve our awareness and our actions. With experience, we will adapt and accelerate.

We make the life-changing decision to be a high performer every morning – well before any competition – choosing to head in the right direction. Training, conditioning and establishing habits add up. This is seeing, being, doing and visioning; it is in front of us and closer than we think.

I hope this book has shown a path you can tune to your world, a path to higher performance for you.

It is a relief that high performance is not about competition, as the beauty of performance appears in every piece of art, dance, sport, speech, or kid playing in the park. Performance is the best communication you can offer at any moment.

The chapters of this book form a performance dashboard.

Performance	Me	Us	It
Exceptional	Conviction 7	Flow 8	Creation 9
High	Values 6	Routine 5	Evidence 4
Developing	Awareness 1	Truth 2	Standard 3

Table 2: The high performer's dashboard

As we travel the dashboard, we start knowing who we are through **awareness** of ourselves and the system we are in (1). We know where we are at any moment because we live in the **truth** and have moved beyond agreement (2). We know what we are aiming for and what it takes to hit the top and have a clear picture of the **standard** we are pursuing (3).

We are moving into higher performance. We collect the right **evidence** to measure how we are going and how fast the gap is closing (4). We focus on the **routine** of action that matters and making it happen rather than rumination and indecision (5). We deepen our perspective of our core **values**, our main purpose for performance and what drives our mission (6).

We are moving into the exceptional performance system. Our mindset has reached a new dimension of deep **conviction** through the system and what our action is proving (7). We have moved into momentum where **flow** is not only at the pinnacle event but in our daily routines and interactions with others (8). Our actions are more often the right action at the right time from us and our support. The future is becoming clear, and we bring ourselves to the place we want to **create** (9). We are not oscillating as in our previous patterns but advancing in our actions and our performance. We are making it happen.

When all the pieces are aligned, and you have done the work, then you live in the world of performance acceleration.

Growing performers with a system

They know who they are.
They know where they are.
They know what it takes.

High Performance

They have proof they are getting there.
They have the right action to get there.
They know what matters.

Exceptional Performance

They know they can get there.
They know what to do and how to do it.
They are making it happen.

Performance	Me	Us	It
Exceptional	Conviction	Flow	Creation
High	Values	Routine	Evidence
Developing	Awareness	Truth	Standard

Table 3: The dashboard fast-track

Once the dashboard system has momentum, nine areas distil into three for daily polishing. Our attention becomes focused on growing and deepening self-awareness, polishing our routine, and the progress towards creating a desired future. This becomes the daily routine and is the accelerator built on the foundation of the performance dashboard.

There's an old story of an airline pilot speaking to passengers mid-flight, 'Ladies and gentlemen, I have good news and bad news. The bad news is we are completely lost, but the good news is we are making good time.' We are all in action, but some are just motion while others are progress. Spotting the difference quickly and clearly is the game-changer for the best performers. At any moment, they know where they are. Whatever your goal, you have exceptional buried inside, and when you know your system and where you are, it is within your grasp.

If you are starting out, take the first step. If you are well into the game, enjoy discovering your next best steps and creating your performance system for life.

Your potential is exceptional, and with a system, your performance is about to catch up.

Onwards.

ABOUT THE AUTHOR

As an athlete, coach, researcher, technologist and leader, Richard has helped people prepare for nine Olympics. He has worked for three countries across more than twenty sports focusing on Olympic performance.

Richard holds a PhD is in physiology and biomedical engineering. He is the founder of several international performance programmes, including Technology and Innovation programmes in the UK and New Zealand, and a Performance Knowledge and Learning programme for NZ Olympic, Winter Olympic and Paralympic teams.

In his research, Richard has examined the differences between medallists and non-medallists across five Olympic cycles. He led the performance-learning reviews and analysis for New Zealand in the four years before their most successful Olympic result in Rio in 2016.

Currently, Richard consults internationally and works with Olympic sports, professional sports, national coaches, and former elite athletes. His work focuses on replacing clutter with clarity, turning complications into simplicity, and helping people move from high potential to high performance.

Richard lives in Dunedin, New Zealand, with his partner Donna and their kids, Oliver, Gracie, Emily-Rose and Leo.

> To find out how Richard can help inspire simplicity and accelerate performance for you and your organisation, visit www.simplify2perform.com

REFERENCES

Argyris, C., & Schon, D. A. (1992). *Theory in Practice*. New York: Jossey-Bass.

Bast, F. (2016). Crux of Time Management for Students. *Resonance*, 71-88.

Campbell, J. (2014). *The Hero's Journey. Collected works of Joseph Campbell*. Novato California: New World Library.

Chippendale, P. (1988, March 2). *Minessence*. Retrieved from Minessence: https://www.minessence.net/default.aspx#.YD0IXGgzaUk

Clear, J. (2018). *Atomic Habits: Tiny changes, remarkable results*. New York: Penguin Random House.

Covey, S. R. (1989). *The Seven Habits of Highly Effective People: Restoring the character ethic*. New York: Simon and Schuster.

Csikszentmihalyi, M. (1990). *Flow: The psychology of optimal experience*. New York: Harper & Row.

Dreyfus, S. E., & Dreyfus, H. L. (1980). *A Five-Stage Model of the Mental Activities Involved in Directed Skill Acquisition.* Washington: Storming Media.

Dweck, C. S. (2006). *Mindset: The new psychology of success.* New York: Random House.

Ericsson, K. A. (1996). Expert and exceptional performance: Evidence of maximal adaptation to task constraints. *Annual review of psychology,* 47(1), 273-305.

Ericsson, K. A. (2008). Deliberate Practice and Acquisition of Expert Performance: A General Overview. *Academic Emergency Medicine,* 15(11), 988-994.

Eurich, T. (2018). What self-awareness really is (and how to cultivate it). *Harvard Business Review.*

Fritz, R. (1989). *The Path of Least Resistance: Learning to become the creative force in your own life.* New York: Fawcett Columbine.

Fritz, R. (2016). *Identity.* Newfane: Newfane Press.

Fritz, R. (2016). *Identity.* Newfane, VT: Newfane Press.

Garrett, N. L. (2016). The brain adapts to dishonesty. *Nature Neuroscience,* 19, 1727–1732.

Gladwell, M. (2005). *Blink: The power of thinking without thinking.* New York: Little, Brown and Co.

REFERENCES

Goffman, E. (1959). *The Presentation of Self in Everyday Life*. New York: Anchor Books.

Harris, R. (2019). ACT Made Simple: An easy-to-read primer on acceptance and commitment therapy. *New Harbinger Publications*.

Hunter, J. P. (2004). Interaction of step length and step rate during sprint running. *Medicine & Science in Sports & Exercise*, 36(2), 261-271.

Kahneman, D. (2011). *Thinking Fast and Slow*. New York: Farrar, Straus and Giroux.

Kim, D. H. (1994). Putting systems thinking into practice. *System Dynamics Review*, 10(2-3), 277-290.

Kim, D. H. (1999). *Introduction to Systems Thinking (Vol. 16)*. Waltham: Pegasus Communications.

Maeng, J. S. (2013). A modeling approach to energy savings of flying Canada geese using computational fluid dynamics. *Journal of Theoretical Biology*, 76.

McDavid, J. (2020). *The Social Dilemma*. Retrieved from Netflix: https://www.netflix.com/nz/title/81254224

Miller, S. S. (2008). *Eagles*. New York: The Rosen Publishing Group.

Nielsen. (2021, March). Retrieved from Gracenote: https://www.gracenote.com/

Oxford Languages. (2016). *Word of the year 2016*. Retrieved from Oxford Languages: https://languages.oup.com/word-of-the-year/2016/

Pennebaker, J. W. (2011). *The Secret Life of Pronouns: What our words say about us*. New York: Bloomsbury Press.

Revans, R. (1980). *Action Learning: New techniques for management*. London: Blond & Briggs.

Senge, P. M. (1997). The Fifth Discipline. *Measuring Business Excellence*.

Wachowski, L. &. (Director). (1999). *The Matrix* [Motion Picture].

CPSIA information can be obtained
at www.ICGtesting.com
Printed in the USA
LVHW071823290721
694063LV00020B/403

9 780473 564704